History of the Fort Worth Legal Community

Ann Arnold

EAKIN PRESS ꟼⅇꝑ Austin, Texas

FIRST EDITION
Copyright © 2000
By Ann Arnold
Published in the United States of America
By Eakin Press
A Division of Sunbelt Media, Inc.
P.O. Drawer 90159 ◫ Austin, Texas 78709-0159
email: eakinpub@sig.net
▣ website: www.eakinpress.com ▣
ALL RIGHTS RESERVED.
1   2   3   4   5   6   7   8   9
1-57168-352-6

For CIP information, please access:
www.loc.gov

Contents

Foreword

Everyone with ties to Fort Worth is always searching for interesting historical accounts of Fort Worth and Tarrant County. The combination of Fort Worth historical references tied into the legal profession makes this book a compelling read.

It would take twenty volumes this size to reference all of the outstanding achievements of the lawyers who have practices in Tarrant County to the present date. This work contains highlights of the careers of some of the most colorful and successful practitioners of law that Tarrant County has known, accompanied by detailed historical accounts of the law schools that have been established in Fort Worth, as well as the history of our courthouses. These accounts would remain lost in our archives but for the author's research and hard work in accumulating them in this volume.

No county in Texas can boast of a richer tradition in the legal profession and judiciary than that of Tarrant County. A book dedicated to highlighting the legal community in Tarrant County has been long overdue.

WADE H. MCMULLEN

Acknowledgments

Many people helped make this book possible and I am grateful to all, but special thanks to Ken Hopkins and his staff at the Fort Worth Public Library Genealogy and Local History Department, and to Gerald Saxon and his staff at the University of Texas at Arlington Special Collections Department. The lawyers interviewed were gracious and shared not only recollections and insight, but personal memorabilia as well. The staff at Texas Christian University and at Texas Wesleyan University School of Law provided photographs which greatly enhance the book.

Judge Steve King allowed me access to personal historical documents concerning the courthouses. Wade McMullen of the Tarrant County Bar Association helped in multiple ways. Both gave me a greater appreciation of the legal community. David Fielding was good enough to assist me with technical advice.

Robyn Weaver and fellow writers in the Writers Group of Fort Worth helped clarify when my prose didn't say what I meant for it to say.

To all of these my heartfelt thanks.

Introduction

Ask members of the bar why they became lawyers and many simply respond that they love the law. But what is the law? It is the tapestry of rules that governs us, woven by a complex society and interpreted and administered by lawyers. *Black's Law Dictionary* lists thirty defining references to the word "law." One is a "general rule of human action, taking cognizance only of external acts, enforced by a determinate authority, which authority is human, and among human authorities is that which is paramount in a political society."[1]

This also defines a legal community, i.e. lawyers, judges, legislators and their day-to-day interactions with the people of a given jurisdiction. Business contracts, real estate transactions, traffic laws—all impact lawyers and laymen on a daily basis. As one steeped in the tradition of the law defined it, "law is the oil that allows society to function."

Sidney L. Samuels, Fort Worth city attorney from 1907 to 1909 and recognized as one of the great lawyers of Texas, wrote, "Law is not a watertight compartment sealed and shut off from contact with the drama of life which unfolds before our eyes. It is in no sense a cloistered realm, but a busy state in which events are held up to our vision and touch our elbows."[2] The intent of this slim volume is to give the reader a glimpse of that stage and its actors, and to share their history.

On the Texas frontier, lawyers came from both North and South to establish themselves as part of growing, vibrant communities. Some had been trained in prestigious law schools of the East, others "read" the law as apprentices to attorneys who may or may not have been legal scholars. Several came to Fort

Worth to participate in the land boom that developed from the settlement of the old Colonial Spanish Land Grant known as the Peters Colony.

At the turn of the twentieth century, many still viewed legal education as nothing more than mastering a craft. This notion slowly gave way to the philosophy that lawyers needed a knowledge of the principles of law. Harvard founded the first law school in 1815. Yale followed in 1826. Midway through that century fifteen law schools had been established. It was at Harvard in 1870 that Dean Christopher C. Langdell introduced a new concept—the case method. Thus was born a system of teaching law through the study of judicial decisions, a method used today in almost every well-recognized law school in the country, including Fort Worth's Texas Wesleyan University Law School.

In spite of the complexity of federal, state, and local laws, our system of jurisprudence continues to settle many different types of legal disputes resulting from modern commercial and social legislation. Without such a system, we would find ourselves like Moses during the Exodus, bogged down in trivial, sometimes not so trivial, discords. As our population increases, so does the number of courts to assure us of our right to justice. From the first court held under an oak tree by a visiting judge, the legal system has grown to more than one hundred municipal, county, state, and federal courts.

It was the law's fairness and protection that fostered democracy as Fort Worth grew from a small fort on a bluff overlooking the Trinity River to a metropolitan city of 500,000. This is the story of the people's creativity and energy as it relates to the legal community.

PART ONE
The Pioneers

The Early Years: 1849-1900

Obviously, Shakespeare's admonition to "kill all the lawyers" was ignored. The 1997-1998 Tarrant County Bar Association Directory lists 1,936 members. This wouldn't be possible without the solitary New Hampshire attorney, Charles A. Harper, who in 1849 settled in the struggling fort on a bluff overlooking the Trinity River. Others followed.

In 1856 the population reached seventy, with one lawyer. By 1860 the village had grown to include 300 residents and five lawyers. At the turn of the new century, 27,000 people called Fort Worth home and 150 lawyers practiced in the city. At the 1997 dedication of the Texas Wesleyan University School of Law, it was noted the numbers had risen to a population of 450,000 served by 3,000 lawyers.[1]

Harper's services were in demand, as the buying and selling of real estate required legal skill to interpret or write contracts. A tintype is one of the few pieces of evidence of the New Englander's sojourn on the raw frontier. Judging from that likeness, Julia Kathryn Garrett, in *Fort Worth: A Frontier Triumph*, noted, "His discerning eyes indicate that he saw much, divulged little, and was capable of deliberate calculations."[2] In an unexpected way, he became part of the lore of Fort Worth history. When anyone in the 1850s asked the location of a good crossing on the Clear Fork of the Trinity, the answer was, "Go out and you'll find the Blue Hole; it's right where the lawyer got baptized."[3] Harper left the settlement about 1860, presumably due to the war between the region of his youth and his adopted home.

In 1853 John Peter Smith joined the hardy pioneers at the fort. Orphaned at the age of thirteen, he lived for a while with a cousin on a farm in Kentucky. Smith attended Bethany College from 1851 until he journeyed westward. He traveled by steamboat to New Orleans, then up the Red River to Shreveport. There he connected with a wagon train bound for Dallas. After calculating his chances of successfully competing against other young men with more money and advantages, Smith opted to move on to the less populous fort town thirty miles to the west. Because he lacked money for the stagecoach fare, he walked. By all accounts he made the right choice. Penniless when he arrived, at the time of his death he was estimated to be worth one million dollars.

As did others of his day and time, John Peter Smith wore a long, full beard. Pictures show him looking like an advertisement for Smith Brothers' Cough Drops.

He first taught school in the new settlement but quit due to poor health. Later, he read law with A. Y. Fowler, "and without attending any law schools was admitted to the bar in 1860."[4] As an attorney, he practiced in both state and federal courts.

Smith and fellow lawyer Dabney Dade voted with Sam Houston opposing secession. But when the war broke out, like others who were philosophically opposed to the rift, he joined the Confederate Army. His cavalry brigade fought mainly in Louisiana.

It was after the Civil War that his deeds led to his being designated the "Father of Fort Worth." A man of many talents, his several occupations included surveyor, teacher, Texas Ranger, and lawyer. He also served as mayor in the 1880s.

In that capacity Smith brought about multiple civic improvements. He led the way for the first street pavings and supported a tax to pay for free public schools. In matters of health, he promoted the building of a sanitary sewer system and initiated a pump station that transformed Trinity River water into potable water at the rate of four million gallons a day.

John Peter Smith died April 11, 1901, while on a business trip to St. Louis. He was eulogized by city leaders J. C. Terrell, C. D. Lusk, and T. N. Edgell, who noted his membership with the Masons and the Christian Church. They wrote, "His life was so gentle, and the elements were so mix'd [*sic*] him, that Nature might stand up, and say to all the world, THIS IS A MAN!"[5]

John Christopher Terrell, a young attorney on his way to the California gold fields in 1857, stopped to visit a friend, Dabney C. Dade, in the sparsely populated village on the Trinity. He liked the invigorating climate, both natural and commercial. The prospect of establishing a successful career appealed to him, so he decided to change plans.

J. C. Terrell was born in 1831 while the family was en route from Virginia to Missouri. As a youth, described as the "wild" child of a wealthy Missouri landowner, Terrell showed no interest in serious study or vocation. But owing to the family's status, his widowed mother insisted he obtain an education. He read law with his brother, Judge Alexander W. Terrell and, at twenty-one, he was admitted to the Missouri bar in 1852.

For two years he practiced law in Santa Clara and Monterrey, California. Occasionally he wandered up to Oregon to take a case. In 1856 he returned to Virginia for a short stay, then on to Austin, Texas, where brother A. W. was a judge. Still without thought to settling down, he left again for California, this time traveling through Fort Worth. The result was the fortuitous meeting with Dade. Terrell, in his book *Reminiscences of the Early Days*, wrote, "We were not long forming the law partnership of Terrell & Dade, which continued here until the beginning of the Civil War."[6]

The two set about opening an office. "Typical of frontier construction," according to historian Oliver Knight, "the combination home and law office built by Terrell and Dade was a single-story building of two rooms, with a fireplace in each."[7] One crude room was the residence of the bachelor friends, the other the law office.

Terrell recalled he and Dade had difficulty meeting proper young ladies. The two loved Sunday school, and decided to start one. Their motives, however, were not totally pious. "We had a prosperous and profitable time, broke the ice and got acquainted with the girls, and Sundays became too short then."[8]

As the two prospered, and the village grew, they moved their offices to more comfortable quarters. When hostilities broke out between the states, Dade returned to the North, Terrell formed a company to fight for the South.

In 1871 Terrell married Mary Lawrence, one of the best educated women in Fort Worth. With his acquired maturity he emerged as one of Fort Worth's preeminent legal minds, maintaining a law office in the same location for twenty-four years.

Buckley B. Paddock, another pillar of the community, was a native of Ohio. At age sixteen he traveled to Mississippi to enlist as a scout in the Confederate army and became one of the youngest officers in the South. After the war Paddock settled in Fayette, Mississippi, where he studied law at night before passing the bar. He lawyered for several years, but a desire to print a newspaper prompted his move to Texas.

In Fort Worth he met with K. M. Van Zandt. Already a community leader, Van Zandt took a liking to the personable youth. Both were to reminisce over that interview:

"'What would you like to do?' Van Zandt asked.

"'I would like to run a newspaper, sir,' Paddock said."[9] Van Zandt just happened to have one, and Paddock became editor and publisher.

He started the *Fort Worth Democrat*. In his adopted home he identified two types of local crime: so-called victimless crimes, i.e. drunkenness, gambling, and prostitution as practiced in Hell's Half Acre; and violent crimes such as assault, robbery, and murder which knew no geographical boundary. He diligently reported them all in his newspaper. Paddock noted that some lawyers' sole practice was defending prostitutes and saloon-keepers, which could be why every law office was within a half-block of a saloon or bordello.

While John Peter Smith was acknowledged as the "Father of Fort Worth," Paddock admitted it fell to him "to foster the child through its village and city development and to live to witness in later times the fine fruition of the plans and enterprises that engaged his earlier associate."[10] He tried to do just that while serving as mayor from 1882 to 1900.

Near the end of his journalistic career, Paddock authored *History of Texas; Fort Worth and the Texas Northwest Edition*. The

B. B. Paddock; lawyer turned newspaper editor.
—Photo courtesy of UTA Special Collections Library

four volume account chronicled the city's early days and actions of its leading founders and citizens.

Hyde Jennings came in 1873—the year Fort Worth was incorporated. He established a successful law practice and became wealthy through his timely land purchases. With Ephriam Daggett, he dedicated the Daggett and Jennings additions "to public use" in 1873. During the period of Hell's Half Acre, the Jennings addition remained relatively free of vice. Not so the Daggett addition, which became known as the wicked district. One way the men were alike, however, was "Both Ephriam Daggett and Hyde Jennings were large, rotund men who enjoyed eating well and making money."[11] Like other lawyers before and after him, Jennings found real estate to be more lucrative than the exclusive practice of law.

As the population increased, so did the need for legal ordinance. Attorney J. Y. Hogsett was called upon to write the City Charter.[12] Hogsett was born July 22, 1843, in Anderson County, Tennessee. At the age of sixteen, having graduated from Union Academy in Clinton, Tennessee, he came to Texas. Except for the time he served in the Confederate army, he remained in Texas for seven years. When the Civil War broke out, he volunteered and served on the New Mexico frontier. The young soldier was stricken with smallpox. When his troop evacuated, he was left behind. Captured by Union forces, he was later paroled. Still weak from his illness and without a horse, he walked to San Antonio, "a terrible foot journey."[13]

Hogsett returned to Tennessee and at the age of twenty-four he read law in the office of Judge D. K. Young, and was admitted to the bar in April 1869.

Three years later he returned to Fort Worth and entered a partnership with Capt. John Hanna. The firm Hanna & Hogsett lasted until December 31, 1880, when it was dissolved by mutual consent. After the partnership, Hogsett practiced alone, specializing in title and land litigation.

Journalist B. B. Paddock described Hogsett as a man whose "habits were of strict sobriety and patient industry."[14] He was one of the organizers and first president of the Fort Worth Life Insurance Company. Later he sold his holdings and devoted himself to his farm, ranch, and real estate investments. His

Powell Building office housed one of the most extensive law libraries in the county. At the time of his death in 1912 the library was valued at over $1,000.

The same year Hogsett came to Fort Worth, the Seventeenth Judicial District, of which Tarrant County was a part, included Dallas, Denton, Parker, and Wise counties. The unpopular Reconstruction governor Edward J. Davis appointed one-armed Hardin Hart presiding judge. Barroom and poker table vernacular was part of his judicial language. In trial, attorney J. C. Terrell proposed to amend his pleadings. Judge Hart responded, ". . . Now, Joe, you know you cannot raise at this stage of the game. Gause (William R.) stands pat on his general denial and you will have to call or lay down your hand."[15]

Like his mentor, Hart, though colorful, was not held in high esteem by lawyers or litigants. Hart in turn was not impressed by the opinions of higher courts. "At one time, James H. Field was arguing a case, when the judge interrupted him and proceeded to render a decision averse to Field's contention. Field, opening a law book, said: 'If your Honor pleases, the Supreme Court says—.'" Hart stopped him in mid-sentence. "Well, let the Supreme Court say it agin [*sic*], if it wants to."[16] Despite his coarseness, he was seldom overturned.

James Jones Jarvis—lawyer, soldier, capitalist, and philanthropist—didn't arrive in Fort Worth until the early 1870s. He began his legal career by reading law at Urbana, Illinois, and, his biographer noted, became acquainted with a lawyer from Springfield. "While Major Jarvis was not of his politics, he remembers with a great deal of pleasure, his intimate acquaintance with Abraham Lincoln, who was then practicing law in Urbana."[17] Lincoln went to Washington, D. C., and Jarvis went to Quitman, Texas.

Caleb Pirtle in *Fort Worth: The Civilized West*, reported the twenty-five-year-old heard Texas needed lawyers. "He decided to find out. It was the winter of 1856. . . . Jarvis arrived with $60. He loaned $55 to a needy friend and began a most successful legal career with only $5 for a new suit and pair of shoes."[18]

He served for two years as judge of Wood County and two years as district attorney for the Sixth Judicial District.

Jarvis harkened to his North Carolina childhood when

called upon to declare his allegiance in the War between the States. He joined the Confederate Army and served in Company A, Tenth Regiment of Texas Cavalry and with Beauregard's Army of Tennessee. Attaining the rank of major, Jarvis was slightly wounded in the battle of Murfeesboro. He was home on furlough when the war ended.

Following his release from the army, Jarvis married Ida Van Zandt, daughter of Isaac Van Zandt. He brought his family to Fort Worth in 1872 and settled them in a three-room cabin on the site later occupied by the Westbrook Hotel. Within five years he built a better home for his growing family, using lumber transported from East Texas by ox-driven wagons. Located at 702 Lamar Street in what was then a genteel neighborhood, the home was one of the first two-story residences.[19] It featured high ceilings, leadedglass windows, and gingerbread moldings.

Major Jarvis joined the firm of Smith and Hendricks in 1872, but the latter died only two months after the association began. Eventually the firm was named Smith, Jarvis and Jennings, with offices in four rooms above the Tidball, Van Zandt & Company Bank.

In the first hectic years, Jarvis' law practice gave him an opportunity to partici-

Attorney James Jones Jarvis is best remembered for his support of Texas Christian University.
—Photo courtesy Fort Worth Public Library Genealogy and Local History Department

pate in numerous business ventures that were organized in the 1870s. It was in the law office which he shared with John Peter Smith that the community leaders organized the Board of Trade on October 24, 1876. The purpose of the Board was to promote and regulate the expanding trade of the area. Thirty-five years later the Board of Trade would play a decisive role in luring Texas Christian University to the city.

Jarvis took advantage of the 1880s boom years to invest heavily in real estate. At the turn of the century he was one of the wealthiest men in the city.

One observer said of Jarvis, "He is a man of sterling worth and strict integrity, who could not swerve from what is right and proper; of unquestioned ability, a lawyer of great power, zealous for his clients, and of fine address at the bar. As a criminal lawyer, he has few superiors."[20]

The distinguished lawyer left his stamp on many civic activities as well. He served as a school trustee and, in that capacity, hired Miss Sue Huffman, the first superintendent of schools. An ardent Democrat, Jarvis was elected to the State Senate in 1886. "Although he had retired from the practice of his profession a number of years prior to his entrance into the Legislature, his exceptional learning and abilities as a lawyer were well known to and recognized by his colleagues."[21] These skills, plus his reputation as a financier, placed him in a leadership role during his tenure.

Jarvis spent his last years either raising cattle and horses on his 5,000-acre ranch ten miles north of Fort Worth or on his 26,000-acre ranch in Hood and Erath counties. Historian Colby Hall and others credit Jarvis with being a driving force in securing educational institutions for the region. "Notwithstanding his record in the field of law, politics and finance, Major Jarvis is no doubt best known to the people of Texas as a whole, and is gratified to be able to base his principal claim to their esteem, because of his active interest in and liberal contributions to the cause of higher Christian education in the State."[22]

Not all citizens were as well respected as Jarvis. Squire B. F. Barkley, a Republican, "found it expedient to be escorted between home and office each day by a bodyguard of Negro soldiery."[23] After Reconstruction, and when he was no longer a judge, B. F. Barkley practiced law. Also, as United States commissioner and land agent, he negotiated contracts for several thousand acres of choice land sales.

Other lawyers of the period included E. P. Albritton, John T. Ault, H. Barksdale, H. G. Bowen, W. M. Campbell, Dan B. Corley, C. C. Cummings, John J. Good, Junius W. Smith, John F. Swayne, and the firm of Hanna and Hogsett. By the end of the 1870s, the legal field was so crowded that several lawyers, like Barkley, advertised their expertise as land agents in addition to their legal work.

As were previous mayors of the young city, R. E. Beckham was an attorney. Prior to coming to Texas, he studied law in Kentucky and in 1866 was admitted to the Calloway County Bar. As did many young men after the Civil War, the former Confederate captain headed west and arrived in Fort Worth in 1873. Beckham set up shop in B. B. Paddock's *Fort Worth Democrat* editorial offices. His advertisement stated he was available for "those in need of an efficient attorney."[24] He and law partner C. C. Cummings were part of a growth spurt in which forty new stores and businesses opened in one year.

Beckham continued his practice of the law and added the duties of mayor five years later. The year was 1878, and reform of widespread vice and corruption was on the voters' minds. Beckham managed to gain the support of both businessmen and church members. As mayor, his idea of reform consisted of cutting the police force to three members, thus saving tax dollars and pleasing businessmen. He supported Sunday closing laws. This appealed to the church crowd. County Attorney N. R. Bowlin supported Beckham's efforts, declaring gamblers would have to go. But actions spoke louder than words. Despite his good efforts, law enforcement was not strict. Customers and merchants in The Acre hardly noticed the difference in administrations.

Beckham was county judge from 1880 to 1884, then served as the first judge of the Seventeenth District Court until 1892. He continued his attempts at reform in those offices. Believing his courtroom was a place for civilized deliberation, he requested that peace officers remove their sidearms when in court. Such a notion was about as welcome as heat rash. He bowed to the will of the lawmen who would as soon appear in public without their weapons as without their pants.

Another unpopular idea put forward was that elected officials should have squeaky clean reputations. In 1889 he directed a grand jury to "look closely into the conduct of all public officials, and let no man escape because of high social or financial standing."[25] This was at a time when delving into the ownership of places in The Acre would embarrass more than one prominent politician. But that public exposure would have to wait until preacher J. Frank Norris came to town.

Judge Beckham died in June 1910. He had witnessed and participated in the evolution of Fort Worth from a frontier village to a prosperous town.

R. L. Carlock was elected county attorney in 1886, replacing Bowlin. Like his predecessor, Carlock joined Beckham in trying to clean up Hell's Half Acre. Their efforts, plus the support of Mayor H. S. Broiles and editor B. B. Paddock, did much to put a lid on open vice and corruption.

By 1890 a new generation of lawyers was having an impact on the city. One, Col. Richard Wynne, was a gubernatorial candidate in 1896. Another, John Rollo Black, moved from Quincy, Illinois, to Fort Worth shortly after the turn of the century. He worked as a bookkeeper at the A. and L. August Clothing Store and studied law by correspondence.

Described as strait-laced and austere, Black was an ordained minister, active in his church, but did not pastor a congregation. Admitted to the Texas Bar in 1907, he practiced here and was a member of the Fort Worth Bar for fifty years. Greatly admired by his peers, he was addressed as Judge Black. According to his daughter, "His real estate holdings included acreage along what is now Grapevine Highway. Black Drive is named for him."[26] He died October 31, 1957, in his eightieth year.

Not all lawyers practiced law. In 1870 George L. Gause left the practice with his father, Col. William R. Gause, to establish the Missouri Wagon Yard. A large part of his business was renting hearses. "In 1879 Fort Worth was a boisterous, rowdy frontier town. But it did possess many amenities of civilization. . . . One thing it did not have, however, was a funeral home."[27] Seeing the need for a mortuary, Gause went East and studied embalming. Upon his return, he and Frank Flenner opened what would become Gause-Ware Funeral Home, later Gause-Ware, Owens and Brumley.

Prior to the establishment of law schools, aspirants to the bar studied with learned men in an apprenticeship structure. Called reading the law, these young men (it was much later that women studied law) researched cases, wrote briefs, and sometimes swept the offices and carried in the coal. One such young man was Carl William Goerte. Born in Fort Worth on January 15, 1887, he attended local schools and read law in the office of Judge George M. Conner. He was admitted to the Texas Bar in 1919 upon his return from the U.S. Army.

Courts also were different back then. In the late 1870s the Tenth District Court met the six Mondays after the first Monday in both February and July. The Criminal Court met the first Monday of each month, and Probate Court held sessions the third Monday of January and each alternate month after that. These Mondays were big social occasions with men coming from throughout the county to visit, whittle, spit, and observe each other and the litigants. That is, unless a cattle drive was rumbling through town.

From April until September it was impossible to hold court with one to two thousand bawling steers trudging down Rusk Street. Not only was the noise deafening, the dust was stifling.

In 1884 the Seventeenth District Court was limited to Tarrant County. A second district court was established in 1891, but the third court would not be needed until after the turn of the century.

As lawyers became more professional and organized, they sought to increase their skills. The *Austin Daily Statesman* noted on Saturday, June 11, 1892, that the Fort Worth Law Library Association filed a charter for the purpose of maintaining a local law library. The venture was capitalized at $25,000.

Another step toward professionalism was the establishment of a law school.

PART TWO
The Law Schools

Fort Worth University

Ring, rah, ru!
Do your do!
Varsity, varsity!
Fort Worth U[1]

"**O**f the educational institutions which have had the greatest influence on Fort Worth, John Peter Smith's first school and the defunct Fort Worth University head the list,"[2] according to Woody Phipps of the WPA Texas Writers' Project. Despite Phipps' glowing pronouncement, Fort Worth University was not the first of its kind. A small school, the Fort Worth Business College located near what is now Sundance Square, offered a variety of courses, including those leading to a diploma in law. It predated Fort Worth University by nine years.

Early on, city fathers recognized the need for a center of higher learning. *The Dallas Herald* reported on July 8, 1871, the first formal meeting to discuss the matter.

> At a Preliminary Meeting of a number of the citizens of Fort Worth and vicinity, called for the purpose of taking into consideration the establishment of a College at Fort Worth.
> On motion J. A. Clark was called to the chair, and Junius W. Smith was requested to act as Secretary.

After the Chairman had explained the object of the meeting it was unanimously

Resolved That a Board of Trustees be elected whose duty it shall be to draft and specify the plan by which the means and money ran [*sic*] be raised in order to procure the grounds and

Fort Worth University Hall, built in 1887.
—Photo courtesy Fort Worth Public Library
Genealogy and Local History Department

erect the building necessary to the permanent establishment of a first class College.

The following were then selected as Trustees, to wit: H. G. Hendrix, K. M. Van Zandt, John P. Smith, R. M. King, E. H. Dagget [*sic*], J. A. Clark, S. Terry S. Evans, and W. H. Overton; and Junius W. Smith was appointed permanent Secretary of the Board of Trustees.

It was resolved that the Trustees shall appoint a financial and traveling agent to solicit subscriptions and scholarships, to receive and collect money, and take such other steps as many be necessary to the permanent establishment of said College.

It was resolved that these proceedings be sent to the *Dallas Herald*, *Weatherford Times*, and *Denton Monitor*, with the request to publish.

J. A. Clark, President
Junius W. Smith, Secretary.[3]

Five of the trustees were lawyers, including Smith, the secretary.

In 1880 city leaders Maj. K. M. Van Zandt, Capt. J. C. Terrell, W. J. Boaz, W. H. Cannon, and H. W. Nye met with delegates of the Methodist Church to secure their backing for the school. Thus what would become Fort Worth University was created.

The city's first "big" college was chartered by the Methodist Church's Northern branch on June 6, 1881. For the next twenty-five years the institution thrived as thousands of North Texas men and women graced its halls. Named for John Wesley, the school was called Texas Wesleyan College, not to be confused with the later college of the same name. In *The New Handbook of Texas, Vol. 2*, a researcher wrote that it was "authorized to maintain the usual curricula and departments of a college and to confer the corresponding degrees." The college's initial classes were held September 7, 1881, in rented space.[4] Ten freshmen and six sophomores, plus 107 academy students, comprised the first class.

Campus and building would come later. A committee was formed "to contract for the brick necessary . . . upon the best terms they may be able to make, after the money is in sight with which to pay for it, and to produce the lumber necessary . . . upon the very best possible rates, when the money is in sight to pay for it."[5] "When the money was in sight to pay for it" was obviously of concern to the committee.

Percival M. White served as president of the fledgling school. The initial excitement did not generate adequate support, and his administration was beset constantly by money problems. After four years A. A. Johnson became president of the college. He introduced an endowment plan, "by which one could purchase a Perpetual Scholarship for $1,000 which entitled the purchaser, his heirs, or his assigns to have free tuition forever in all departments."[6] It held at bay the wolf pawing outside the door for a few more years.

The first classrooms were housed in temporary buildings on the corner of Jennings Avenue and Eleventh Street. Five years later, having outgrown its original site, the school moved further south, to what is now the campus of Green B. Trimble High School. The *Fort Worth Weekly Gazette* announced, "The plans and specifications for the Fort Worth University have been adopted and bids for the work are being asked for."[7] The article went on to say the main building would be 160 feet across the front, eighty feet deep, and three stories high, with a grand tower in the center. Seal brown stones would be used. At a cost of $100,000, the *Gazette* predicted it would be one of the finest educational structures in the Southwest.

In honor of its new location, city fathers named the neighboring street College Avenue. A post card, with a one cent stamp and addressed to Mrs. P. W. Brown, Palestine, Texas, pictured the three-story brick building. A windmill and water tank are visible in the background. Their importance was underscored by the notice to students to use water very sparingly, as the cost was one cent per barrel.

Young Texans paid less than $200 a year tuition. Those not living at home could get a room for fifty cents a week, bumped up to $3.00 if meals were included.

Dr. George W. Gray of Chicago, head of the Methodist Southern Education Society, visited early in 1889. In a nostalgic piece on the old school, a *Fort Worth Star-Telegram* writer declared the trip "convinced him (Gray) TWC should be expanded, and the school opened for the September term under a new charter naming it Fort Worth University."[8]

The school's reputation and student body grew in tandem with the overall growth of the city. By 1888 more than 900 collegians studied in the seven buildings. The faculty numbered forty-seven. A photograph of the period shows three magnificent stone and brick buildings: Cadet Hall, Science Hall, and University Hall. Cadet Hall was a dormitory for boys, and as the name implies, they were subjected to military discipline. The Science Hall housed experimental laboratories, a museum, and the gymnasium. The crown jewel of the campus was University Hall. In it were the president's office, classrooms, music practice rooms, chapel, library, and art studio.

Brochures extolling the virtues of higher education noted the school's offerings of Greek, Latin, Christian evidence and English Bible, music, art, oratory, philosophy, and a school of pedagogy. The coed institution provided military training for boys and "homelike accommodations for girls."[9] The *University Unit*, a monthly newspaper published by students, was "a very good source of chatty information about campus life."[10] The *Unit* cost one dollar a year, payable in advance.

Not all activities were in the classrooms. President Oscar Fisher designated space for baseball and football fields. In a game with Polytechnic College, an opposing player tackled future lawyer George Steere, breaking his leg. Outraged, "Fisher publicly stated that he was not going to allow his young gentlemen to play with a crown [*sic*] of roughnecks, and this incident stopped football at the university for a time."[11]

A school of law was established at Fort Worth University in August 1893, with President Fisher also serving as law school president. Faculty included Dean O. S. Lattimore, C. R. Bowlin, and R. H. Buck. *News-Tribune* writer Mack Williams noted, "Lattimore and Buck later became well-known judges."[12]

A medical school was organized the following year.

Students enrolled in courses in the school of arts and sciences which offered such degrees as A.B., B.Litt., B.S., and Ph.D. A four-year program led to the M.D. degree. Three years of study were needed for the LL.B. "By the standards of that day it was one of the great schools of the Southwest," according to Millhouse in *Oklahoma City University*.[13]

The *Lasso*, the university's 1898 yearbook, pictured student life on the campus: women in ankle-length dresses, men in high, stiffly-starched collars and bowler hats. Evergreens about six feet high and a few spindly trees dotted the landscape. George W. Steere, W. M. Short, and J. R. Stitt were on the *Lasso* staff.

In the flowery language of the Victorian period, the yearbook's dedication read, "To our esteemed President, whose unfaltering purpose and untiring efforts has [*sic*] secured for Fort Worth University such unquestioned merit and high standing, as to make the coming of its many victories possible, and whose enthusiastic devotion in his chosen field has given to higher education in Texas as so great a stimulus—to President O. L. Fisher, A.M.D.D., the *Lasso* is affectionately dedicated."[14] Fisher is pictured with longish, thinning hair brushed behind his ears and a full mustache dominating his face.

The law school's Class of '99 had the motto "We are a law unto ourselves." Officers included men who would serve the community well in the twentieth century. Raymond Buck was president; John R. Robinson, vice-president; John Story, treasurer; W. O. Morton, secretary; and W. M. Short, was historian.

While the university was educating Fort Worth youth, the city experienced enormous post-Civil War growth. The great cattle drives, which were to become the basis of many sagas, were real to the merchants who supplied the trail drivers. Ray Miller, in his *Eyes of Texas* series, commented, "The cattle business assumed even more importance when Armour and Swift both built major packing plants adjacent to the Fort Worth Stockyards in 1902."[15]

The Texas and Pacific Railroad was also a prime employer. Due to the vast amount of business generated by large commercial interests and litigation with the railroads, it became necessary to create three district courts for Tarrant County. More courts meant more opportunities for university law students.

Increased commerce created sufficient money for Texas families to send their sons and daughters to Fort Worth University. The booming rise in population assured these graduates jobs to meet the needs of the people. As the nineteenth century drew to a close, the ragged edge of frontier life gave way to a more polite social structure as evidenced by the increased potency of the women's movement in daily activities. In all of this activity and growth, Fort Worth University played a key role.

Yet the turn of the century did not bode well for the university. Polytechnic College on the eastern rim of the city had been established by the Northwest Texas Conference of the Episcopal Church, South, in 1890. Less than twenty years later Texas Christian University moved from Waco to west Fort Worth. Both proved to be formidable rivals. By 1905 when William Fielder served as president, the faculty had shrunk to eighteen professors.

The university enjoyed an excellent reputation but lacked financial security. Unable to weather the competition from the two new schools, drastic measures had to be taken. Board minutes of the April 9, 1911, meeting revealed, "Trustees voted to close the school at the end of the spring term, to offer the property for sale, and to distribute its assets between Port Arthur Collegiate Institute, a Swedish Academy at Austin, and the Methodist university which was to open that fall in Oklahoma."[16] This followed the unsuccessful attempt to merge with Polytechnic College in 1910. Six weeks later the *Fort Worth Record* noted, "With the close of the twenty-ninth annual commencement of Fort Worth University at St. Paul's Methodist Church Thursday night, the history of that institution in this city closed."[17]

With the closing of the university, Judge R. H. Buck, who had taught there, started a private school to train lawyers.

The Methodist Church moved the school first to Guthrie, Oklahoma, then merged it with Oklahoma City University.[18] The Dulaney-Browne Library on that campus houses the archives of the old university. Scott Baker, a resident of Saginaw, Texas, in a letter to Fort Worth librarian Ken Hopkins, listed a bound volume of *The University Unit* (1899) and *The Lasso* (1897-1898) as available for researchers. Other volumes include minute records, faculty payroll ledgers, and catalogues.[18]

The Fort Worth Independent School District acquired the property of the defunct institution. The old Central High School opened in 1918 in what had been University Hall. Later it was known as Paschal High School. Still later, re-named Green B. Trimble Technical High School, the site at 1003 W.

Cannon has seen more changes than just the name as it shifted from university to academic high school to vocational/technical high school.

Although the university moved to Oklahoma, many of its alumni remained. There were several graduates of the law school whose influence was felt in the first half of the century.

One was John Madison Mothershead, who moved with his family from Panola County, Mississippi, to Texas after the Civil War. He attended local schools, including Fort Worth University. Mr. Mothershead was admitted to the bar in 1895 and practiced law in Tarrant County until 1910. For ten years he worked in San Saba, then returned to Fort Worth and stayed until 1926. His forty-five-year career as an attorney ended with his death in 1940. At that time he was a resident of Harlingen and past director of the Cameron County Bar Association.

Robert Franklin Peden, born on a farm in Parker County in 1880, was a 1907 graduate of the university. He practiced law in Fort Worth from 1907 to 1919, then moved to El Paso where he joined his brother in the firm of Peden and Peden. They later moved to Houston where Robert was active in Harris County Democratic Party campaigns, served on the executive committee, and was a presidential elector in 1948. He served two terms as president of the Houston Bar Association and held memberships in several civic organizations. At the time of his death in 1954, Peden had practiced law for forty-seven years.

William M. Short served as a class officer and graduated from Fort Worth University School of Law in 1898. Admitted to the Texas Bar in 1899, he began his long career in the offices of Williams Capps and S. B. Cantey. He was made partner in the venerated firm of Capps, Cantey, Hanger and Short. Active in numerous church and civic endeavors, he served as president of the Fort Worth Board of Education. The Danville, Illinois, native died June 19, 1948, three days short of his seventy-fourth birthday. His law practice spanned the years from 1899 to 1947.

Another graduate, Chicago-born George W. Steere, was a lover of books. He attended Dallas public schools and received his bachelor of arts degree from Fort Worth University, where he served as editor-in-chief of the *University Unit*. Steere read law in the offices of Matlock, Miller and Dycus prior to being admitted to the bar in 1901. Still in his thirties, he served as judge of the city court of Fort Worth and also worked as an assistant district attorney handling tax collections. Later, he returned to oversee domestic relations cases in that office.

In 1945 Steere became head of the Tarrant County Law Library at a salary of $175.00 a month. Located on the third floor of the courthouse, the library boasted a collection of more than 7,000 volumes. Prior to the grand opening of the new facilities, Steere was responsible for dusting, repairing, and sorting books that had been stacked in every stray corner and hallway.

Like other Fort Worth University graduates, Steere was active in community affairs. His lifelong interest in books caused him to serve as a member of the board of trustees of the Carnegie Public Library of Fort Worth for more than a quarter of a century. He was also Democratic Party county chairman and active in the Boy Scouts of America. His obituary in the *Texas Bar Journal* read, "Death ended the 47-year legal career of George W. Steere on May 6, 1948, twenty-two days before his seventy-third birthday."[19]

Another class officer was J. W. Stitt. Immediately after graduating as valedictorian of Westminster College in Covington, Tennessee, he moved to Fort Worth. In 1895 the new Texan taught school for three years while studying law at night, specializing in civil cases. He was admitted to the bar in 1900 and gave up his teaching position. The *Texas Bar Journal*, in December 1953, noted, "Stitt began practice of law in 1901 and a short time later was elected to the Fort Worth school board."[20] He became supervisor of the federal census for Tarrant, Denton, and Wise counties during Franklin D. Roosevelt's first term.

In addition to his civic and professional interests, Stitt was active in the Presbyterian Church. Elders remembered him as the organizer of a men's Bible class which he served as its teacher for fifty-three years. Stitt died at the age of eighty-eight.

One of the best known graduates of Fort Worth University School of Law was John Joseph Hurley. Born to Irish immigrant parents on December 12, 1889, he was the first infant christened at St. Patrick's Catholic Church in downtown Fort Worth. While in his teens, eager to be on his own, Hurley worked in Birmingham, Alabama, and began studying law at night.

A graduate of Fort Worth's St. Ignatius Academy and Central High School, he returned to his home city and continued the study of law at Fort Worth University. Hurley was admitted to the bar in 1910. At age nineteen he was the youngest lawyer in the state to pass the bar exam.

Hurley practiced law until he enlisted in the Army in 1917. He attended officers training school and was commissioned a second lieutenant. Following the war he was active in the American Legion.

After his stint in the military, Hurley, known to friends as "Mickey," practiced law for twenty-five years before entering city government.

He was hired June 5, 1935, as director of projects. His main duty was to expedite federal projects, especially in the area of transportation. In a *Fort Worth Press* story in 1960, Hurley explained, "In the depression days of the 1930s, when President Roosevelt started all those alphabet government agencies, I became special agent for the city and travelled a good deal to Washington."[21] Senator Tom Connally introduced World War I hero, Gen. John J. "Blackjack" Pershing, to his fellow Texan. The two became friends, and when the general was traveling in the state he made it a point to visit here.

While employed by the city, Hurley also served as secretary to the Civil Service Board, on the Municipal Civilian Defense Council, and the New Deal PWA and WPA programs. He headed the local drive to raise funds for victims of infantile paralysis. He was a charter member and first president of the Fort Worth Zoological Society.

Hurley retired in 1959 after many years as city personnel director. His major legacy from that position was the establishment of Civil Service guidelines for firemen and policemen.

Upon his retirement from the city in 1959, his office staff presented him with a fishing rod and reel. In addition to fishing, he maintained he would practice law on a limited basis. Hurley died in 1966, seventy-eight years old, and one of the last alumni of Fort Worth's first "real" law school.

Fort Worth University Faculty

James Anderson	E. J. Green
Elias J. Beall	W. R. Howard
Frank D. Boyd	Robert L. Short
Ira C. Chase	Helen M. Stoddard
Alice Conkling	Ida Turner
William Fielder	W. W. Van Grundy
Charlotte E. Fisher	W. B. West
Theodore F. Graham	Ida Williams[22]

Trustees of Fort Worth University

Rev. L. H. Carhart	J. S. Hetherington
Rev. J. B. Holloway	Rev. A. H. Eat
J. C. Terrill	Rev. E. O. McIntyre
John A. Manus	I. W. Rouse
Rev. M. A. Daugherty	W. H. Cannon
Rev. A. A. Johnson	William J. Boaz
Rev. C. W. Hargitt	P. M. White
J. B. Wilde	J. R. Wolf[23]

Class of 1897 School of Law

Jack Clyde	Archibald McCall
Whitmore Morris	Thomas Ridgeway
Tillman Sydnor	

Class of 1899

Raymond Buck	G. E. McGinnis
Harry McGown	W. O. Morton
William M. Short	Bert Stanley
W. Storer	J. C. Taylor[24]

Non-Traditional Study of the Law

Not all students learned the law on a university campus. The old *Fort Worth Record* noted "Fort Worth now has a law school with more than twenty pupils and two professors."[1] One of the professors was Raymond H. Buck. In 1915, as a member of the city legal department, Buck temporarily occupied the police court bench, as well as teaching law in the evening. He and attorney T. R. James, Jr. held classes each Wednesday night in James' American National Bank building offices.

The students ranged in age from youth right out of high school to men in their forties. While never having a formal site, the classes became known as the Fort Worth Night Law School.

The school was the outgrowth of the need to provide greater experiences for those who had been studying the law on their own. The idea of a night law class originated, the newspaper reported, when students "got together and decided that the 'moot' court was a poor way to study law, and personal instruction was the thing needed."[2]

R. H. Buck, later judge of the Court of Civil Appeals, was a prominent member of the legal community. Not only did he impact students, the Buck family drew on his influence. Son Raymond E. Buck became an attorney, as did Raymond E., Jr., and Raymond E., III. The latter, known as "Billy," is an attorney in

Washington, D.C. Raymond E. Buck, Sr. was very active in state and national politics. When he died in 1964, Lyndon B. Johnson was an honorary pallbearer.

Judge Buck's courtroom behavior shows how he may have handled his classes. The judge could be strict when he felt his decrees were violated. For example, he held four newsmen in contempt for failure to disclose the source behind the leak of a grand jury report. J. O. Abernathy, assistant managing editor of the *Fort Worth Record*, Joe J. Fox, and Claude McCaled, *Record* reporters, and Charles F. Pekor, Jr., *Star-Telegram* reporter, were jailed briefly on Buck's orders. The flap arose when "extras" were on the street before he had officially handed down the grand jury indictments.

A Texas Writers' Project author, in recounting the story, quoted an irate jurist. "Judge Buck said that the information furnished the newspapers prematurely was in violation of the law and declared he would ferret out the courthouse official or officials who had violated their oaths of secrecy."[3] The hot story concerned the indictments against R. L. (Bob) Rogers, who was charged with trying to bribe former County Judge R. E. Bratton.

R. H. Buck—lawyer, teacher, judge.
—Photo courtesy Tarrant County Bar Association archives

Buck also could violate his own edicts. He was frequently known to smoke with the lawyers arguing a case before him. But his 1909 New Year's resolution banned smoking in his court room while court was in session. This was contrary to a custom that had prevailed in Tarrant County ever since the establishment of courts. During a January trial, several persons in the court room were smoking cigars. He ordered them to throw away their stogies. They obeyed.

Ten minutes later, the opposing lawyers needed to confer. The story continued, "He then descended from the bench and complacently lighted a cigarette, and puffed away until the conference was over."[4]

Buck's fellow instructor in the night school, T. R. James, Sr., practiced law in partnership with George M. Conner, who was a part-time instructor at the TCU Law School. His father had been named chief justice of the Civil Court of Appeals in 1898, and in 1940 George M. Conner carried on the family tradition. He was chosen to sit as the judge of the 17th District Court in the absence of Frank P. Culver, Jr. who was with the 36th Division as an artillery commander.

Another who taught, but not at a law school, was William Laurence Coley. The Pike County, Illinois, native enjoyed a long and controversial career as both attorney and judge. He entered Eureka College, then taught school for three years. While teaching, he studied law at night. Before coming to Fort Worth, Coley practiced in his home state, Missouri, and Washington, D.C. He moved to Fort Worth in 1919 and was part of the legal community as attorney, law professor, and judge.

In late 1936 Coley was chosen by the city council over six other applicants to serve as judge of the city's corporation court at a salary of $200 a month. He held the position from April 1937 until September 1938. No reason behind the city council's request that he resign was given in his brief statement. "At the request of your body, conscious of no neglect of duty, I hereby resign as corporation court judge of the City of Fort Worth, effective at your pleasure."[5] But the storm clouds had been swirling since January.

In early 1938 Judge Coley contended a dramatic drop in revenues was due to the lack of prosecution of appeals. Court records did not support his argument. City secretary E. S. Birdsong presented figures showing fewer than half the number of appeals were filed during the eight months Coley had been on the bench. Birdsong's data showed 375 appeals versus 974 for Coley's predecessor for a comparable period.

The bottom line was money. The *Star-Telegram* zeroed in on the figures. Traffic fines collected by Judge Coley averaged slightly less than $1.90, compared to the previous average of $2.20. "During the same eight months, revenues from fines collected by the court dropped $9,985 below the amount collected by Coley's predecessor in the corresponding period."[6] The disparity between fines in criminal cases was even greater, from $10.12 to $6.08.

Both before and after his stint at corporation court, he practiced law from his downtown offices. In addition to teaching law in his office at night, he was a devout churchman who taught Bible classes all his adult life. After being seriously injured when he fell against a steam heater at his home in late 1956, Coley retired. In 1962 Coley died eight days before his eighty-seventh birthday.

George Gordon Faust was a student of Judge Coley. Faust was born on a plantation near Lexington, Georgia, in 1890. He moved to Texas after high school and attended Southern Business College. While working as a bookkeeper at Burton-Lingo Lumber Company, he studied law at night. After passing the bar exam, Faust rose from assistant manager of the local yard office to general counsel. He spent the remainder of his career there, "and he was also a director of the company at the time of his death."[7]

Several other students of these night school instructors became well-known attorneys. One, Henry O. Gossett, born in Camden, Arkansas, in 1877, and later a 1916 graduate of the Fort Worth Night School of Law, practiced in Odessa and Longview as well as Fort Worth. Gossett held several judicial positions. "He was judge of the Corporation Court of Fort Worth from 1919 to 1922 and served as judge of the County Court at Law, for civil matters, for two years."[8] In 1930 Judge Gossett moved to Longview where he practiced law until his retirement in 1959.

Baylor B. Brown graduated from the Fort Worth Law School in 1916. He was born in Ranger and attended Hardin-Simmons University and the University of Texas before moving to Fort

Worth. Like several other men in his class, he had business experience prior to getting his law diploma. Brown was secretary to the superintendent of the Texas and Pacific Railroad in Big Spring from 1910 to 1913. Then he worked in the law department of Cattlemens Trust Co. until 1915. After passing the bar, he was associated with Wynn, Irby, Brown, McConnico & Mack.

In World War I he was a second lieutenant in the army, serving in France and promoted to major before his discharge. He was active in veterans affairs, serving as president of the Veterans Service Center, president of the Fort Worth Reserve Officers Association, and a commander of the American Legion.

Sounding like a divorce action, *Brown v. Brown*, Baylor ran against Marvin H. Brown, Sr., for the 1942 Democratic nomination for associate justice of the Second Court of Civil Appeals. He lost, and his future appearances were before, rather than from, the bench.

A classmate of Brown's was Henry R. Bishop. He was the son of Fire Chief Frank Bishop, and as a boy he served as mascot for the old Fort Worth Police Band. Crippled since age eight with a bone disease that caused his right leg to be shorter than the left, he nevertheless was active in Central High School activities and was an able trial lawyer. Except for a brief stint in the 1920s when he worked for District Attorney Marshall Spoonts, Bishop's entire career was in criminal law. For eighteen months prior to his death, poor health led him to curtail his practice to half days. He died of a heart attack in 1949 at the age of fifty-seven.

Night school proved essential for William F. Patterson, who dreamed of becoming a lawyer, but needed to work to make his living. A nationwide trend in the labor movement allowed him to begin his law studies in 1918. Railroad employees, and he was one of them, had just won the right to work an eight-hour day. Under the guidance of R. E. Rouer, night school student Patterson passed the bar examination in 1920. The Alabama native had come to Texas as a young man in 1898 and stayed to practice civil law until 1953.

Another graduate was Julian A. Sory. After serving in the navy, he attended Lon Morris Junior College and Fort Worth Night Law School. He practiced with the firm of Stewart,

Burgess & Morris. During World War II he was with the legal divisions of the Office of Price Administration and the Veteran's Administration. Following the war he returned to Stewart Title Guaranty Company and became active in the Presbyterian Church. He died in 1970 at the age of seventy-three.

Victor H. Lindsey was another of the bright young men who studied law at night. A native of Justin in Denton County, he passed the bar in 1924. For four years he practiced in Fort Worth and served as assistant city attorney. In 1928 he moved to Lubbock, where he again served as assistant city attorney. At the time of his death in 1967, he was presiding judge of the Ninth Administrative Judicial District. Prior to that Lindsey had been judge of the Seventy-second Judicial District Court for twelve years.

The unofficial school led by Buck and James proved there was a need in the North Texas area for a law school. They continued to offer night classes, but in 1917 E. R. Cockrell assumed the lead in traditional legal education for Fort Worth.

Texas Christian University School of Law

With the removal of Fort Worth University to Oklahoma City, North Texans were required to travel to Austin or other cities to attend a university with a law school. Those trips ended in 1915 when the aspiring, cordial Egbert R. Cockrell prevailed upon TCU trustees to again consider a law school.

The Montana native had joined the faculty in 1899. His first attempt to establish a law school occurred the following year when the university was still in Waco. The 1900-1901 catalog announced a full law curriculum with a faculty of three teachers and six guest lecturers. Cockrell and two practicing attorneys, Sam E. Stratton and John J. Foster, were named to lead students to the LL.B. degree upon the completion of a two-year course of study. The catalog promised more than the school could deliver.

It was a bad year for all departments. Enrollment dropped from 161 to 148, and the 1903 catalog made no mention of a law school.

Texas Christian University's history had literally been that of a school on the move. Addison and Randolph Clark, two ministers in the Disciples of Christ Brotherhood, and their sister Ida, established a private school in 1869. The one-room Fort

Worth venture housed six students. Four years later, the Clarks, perhaps the first to flee urban blight, moved the school away from "the alluring vices of the city...."[1] They chose Thorp Spring in Hood County and founded the Add-Ran Male and Female College. After struggling for a dozen years in that location, the brothers, facing bankruptcy, turned the school over to the Disciples of Christ Brotherhood in 1889, and it was renamed Add-Ran University.

That body, with the help of a $35,000 donation from J. J. Jarvis, moved it to Waco six years later and renamed it Add-Ran Christian University. Trustees changed the name to Texas Christian University in 1902. TCU flourished until a fire on March 22, 1910, destroyed the buildings. Dallas, Gainesville, and McKinney made competitive bids to help re-build the university. Historian Caleb Pirtle revealed, "Fort Worth offered fifty-six acres of land, $200,000 in cash, and an assurance that public utilities and streetcar lines would be extended to the campus."[2] The package, better than those offered by the other cities, plus the previous ties to the city, convinced the trustees to award the prize to Fort Worth.

J. J. Jarvis was a major factor in swaying the trustees. B. B. Paddock noted, "Major Jarvis contributed a large sum toward securing for Fort Worth the Texas Christian University, and has since endowed a chair at this university with $15,000."[3]

In 1911 the school moved to its present site in southwest Fort Worth. At the time of the campus relocation, what is now the beautiful TCU neighborhood was hardly more than a bare prairie at the outskirts of the community. But the university was ambitious, and the medical school, started in 1894, continued to be part of the Fort Worth curriculum.

Professor Cockrell moved with the university and persuaded then President Frederick D. Kershner and the trustees to approve a Department of Law. Cockrell, his Woodrow Wilson style pince-nez perched on his Grecian nose, was enthusiastic about the prospect of teaching in his chosen field. However, the trustees gave limited financial support, and Cockrell set out to build a department with very little money. He immediately added Milton E. Daniels and George M. Conner as part-time instructors. The university minutes reflect the bare-bones beginning in that, "Each of these was obligated to secure as many as fifteen students."[4]

Daniels, an athlete as well as a lawyer, was well-liked by the student body. Of Judge Conner it was said if a student survived his classes, he or she definitely knew the law. Cockrell, in addition to teaching and mentoring his law students, maintained his position as head of the Political and Economic Sciences Department.

A student could enroll in a joint undergraduate program and the School of Law, thereby achieving in six years both the B.A. and the LL.B. degrees. The first year of operation fifteen students enrolled; the number grew to seventeen the next two years and jumped to forty-three in 1918. The new department also allowed students to stand for the bar examination after two years of preparation, or continue their studies elsewhere. They were assured any law school to which they might transfer would give credit toward the LL.B. degree.

The Skiff, the student newspaper, reported on January 29, 1915, that students had organized the Texas Christian University Bar Association. Its stated purpose was to keep the students united by meeting frequently to encourage each other and discuss mutual interests. The club was open to men and women taking law courses, or those who intended to make law their profession. *The Horned Frog,* TCU's yearbook, pictured twelve young men as charter members, with Professor Cockrell as sponsor. In the 1920 yearbook, thirty-one young men were pictured as members.

Cockrell chaired the Department of Law and orchestrated the two-year program. His goal was to build a curriculum that would be recognized as equal to that offered at the University of Texas and be accepted by any law school in the country. Qualified sophomores and freshmen could take courses and receive credit toward the bachelor of arts degree. Others could take the examination preparatory to bar admittance.

"In 1917 the program was extended to three years and led to the LL.B. degree," according to Jerome Moore, in *TCU: A Hundred Years.*[5] This was important because students in the three-year program could be admitted to the bar without further examination. The three-year degree came about through the efforts of Professor Cockrell, who lobbied the state legislature to pass the necessary bill. For the first time the TCU Law School was on a par with the University of Texas. Horned Frogs and city fathers were jubilant.

The following year the department was designated as the School of Law with Cockrell as dean. The Law Library was expanded, and entrance requirements were upgraded. Trustees declared the Law School a success.

A practice court was set up to give students realistic experience. The first case "tried" was a "felony" with students John Sturgeon presenting the plaintiff's case and J. A. Raley, Jr. pleading for the defense. The second trial, a civil action, saw Jewell Bauldwin for the plaintiff and Jesse Martin representing the defendant. These trials were followed by several "murder"

C. R. Cockrell

Our Class Professor

"He stands for that which is good."

*Professor E. R. Cockrell,
Texas Christian University
School of Law.*
—Photo courtesy TCU
Communications Dept.

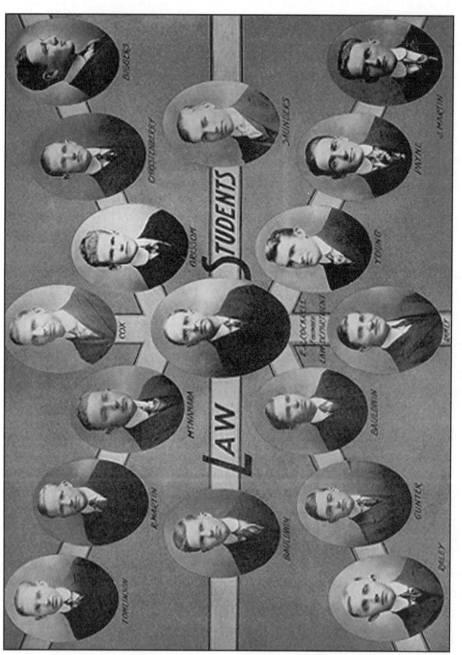

Texas Christian University School of Law.
—Photo courtesy TCU Communications Dept.

trials later in the semester. The "murder" trials, open to all students, were well attended. Regular rules of evidence were strictly enforced by faculty members who supervised the proceedings.

The school prospered until World War I kept away many potential students. Dean Cockrell noted in the spring of 1918 that TCU, like universities across the country, felt the pinch. "Its faculty and its student body are thoroughly patriotic, and each has given its number to our army," he wrote in *The Skiff*.[6] He estimated that half of the 1917 Law School student body was in the military. For those in the army, individual studies, especially classes in military, international, elementary, and commercial law, were made available.

The practice of law was essentially a male-dominated profession, and many of the male students had gone to war. Geneva Bradley, daughter of Judge J. C. Bradley, made the news in September 1917. *The Skiff* headlined "TCU HAS A LADY LAW STUDENT." The story related that the male students still in school expressed themselves as being pleased with the change. But the reporter noted, "It is needless to say that it adds a certain amount of stimulus to the work, for the young men, when they feel that there is a young lady in the class who is likely to show them up in their chosen work at any time."[7] The 1919 yearbook pictured yet another female student among the male Bar Association members.

Four students received the degree of bachelor of laws in 1918. It was the only year the school had a graduating class. Jewell H. (Shorty) Bauldwin of Cleburne, William E. Bauldwin also of Cleburne, Jesse Arna Raley, Jr. of Bryson, and Jesse E. Martin of Fort Worth held that distinction. Martin, after graduation, was awarded a Cambridge University Law School scholarship offered by the United States government to American lawyers in Marine service. After studying in England, he returned to his hometown. He became district attorney ten years later.

Following the war, Dean Cockrell pointed out the need for a first-class law school in the North Texas area. He reported to a citizens' committee that schools normally having up to one hundred students had been severely hurt by the enlistment of students. With peace declared, he anticipated that TCU, although newer, could attract its share of returning veterans. True, some students resumed their studies at the university. But it proved to be too little, too late.

The requirements for TCU's Medical Department, outlined in a February 16, 1917, letter from the American Medical Association, were beyond the financial resources of the university, and the department was disbanded. Three years later the same fate would befall the law school.

The trustees acted June 8, 1920. The School of Law would be abolished, leaving only a pre-law program. It was a controversial decision, with many students, alumni, and others not understanding the reasons behind the action. A page one story in the September 17, 1920, student newspaper clarified the situation by publishing a statement by the board of trustees.

> Attention of Patrons, Old Students and Prospective Students of the Law Department of Texas Christian University:
>
> Gentlemen:
> We are submitting herewith the final decision of the Board of Trustees of Texas Christian University relative to the continuance of the Law Department. This matter was discussed very fully at the February meeting of the Board with a full quorum present. A committee was appointed, consisting of Judge R. M. Rowland, Van Zandt Jarvis, S. J. McFarland, James Harrison, Dean Cockrell, dean-elect of the University, and the President. This committee was to go over the situation carefully and report to the meeting of the Board in June. A meeting of the committee was held and an earnest effort was made to discover all the information necessary to enable it to reach a just and satisfactory decision, and if possible to make a favorable report to the Board relative to the continuance of the Law Department. The committee found in its investigations that satisfactory progress had been made in the development of a Law Department in the last three years, but that the standards of professional education had been raised to the point where it would require a considerable investment, which the Board was not at this time prepared to make, in order to give secure recognition and stability to this department.[8]

One of the standards required a law library of at least 10,000 volumes. TCU's had 2,500. It further required the employment of three, preferably four, instructors whose salary ranged from $3,000 to $3,500 annually. Moreover, all instructors must be members of the Association of American Law Colleges. Regarding students, all candidates for degrees must have two full years of college work, and no candidate for any law degree could be admitted until this requirement was met. The committee estimated it would cost $18,000 to $20,000 a year to maintain the Law Department.

The trustees further noted that to meet the proposed standards it would be necessary to weaken considerably the Department of Political Science and Government. "Not being able to finance same under existing conditions," they said, "we deem it best and advisable to discontinue the Law School."[9]

Colby Hall, in *History of Texas Christian University*, noted that many colleges crippled or killed themselves by undertaking everything that any other college did, regardless of their chances to succeed. Texas Christian University was tempted to follow that path, but after its failed attempts to provide medical and legal programs, the university entered a period of conservation and enhancement of its core curricula. Hall wrote, "One fact has become apparent through the years: T.C.U. was wise in its policy of concentration upon the scope of work it could handle with high quality."[10]

During the school's short existence, noted attorneys Marvin H. Brown, Morris Rector, R. M. Rowland, P. E. Stearns, and E. M. Tipton served as visiting law instructors. By the time of the school's demise, Congressman Fritz Lanham, eight judges, and ten attorneys had taught there. Judge R. H. Buck, of the Court of Appeals, second district, was one of them. Judges Marvin H. Brown and F. O. McKinsey shared their expertise with TCU students. Judge Ocie Speer, whose book served as a text, lectured on women's law.

In 1921 Dean Cockrell obtained a leave of absence from his teaching duties. Historian Colby Hall recalled, "He had specialized in the study of Municipal Law and Administration, so in order to apply his knowledge he announced as a candidate for Mayor of the city of Fort Worth in 1921."[11] As mayor his legacy in that office was to lead the city from the commissioner form of government into a city manager form.

Following his stint in office, Cockrell moved to Fulton,

Missouri, and became president of William Woods College. It would be up to others to carry on the tradition of preparing young men and women for the bar.

One of his colleagues in city government was Rhinehart E. Rouer, who at one time had been on the faculty of the TCU Law School. Rouer, following his teaching career, became one of Fort Worth's most capable city attorneys.

Rouer was at different times a professor at Texas Christian University and also taught in Fort Worth's night law school. "Lanky, but not cranky," was the unofficial 1919 TCU yearbook description of Professor Rhinehart Rouer. The third man to be hired as assistant to Dean E. R. Cockrell, he was well liked by students and respected by faculty.

Rouer was born in Aledo, Texas, in 1890, but his family moved to Fort Worth when he was three years old. He attended Fort Worth schools and graduated from Central High School. Rouer received his law degree from the University of Texas and was admitted to the bar in 1914.

The next year he began his long legal career as a member of the firm Mercer, Wall & Rouer. From 1916 until 1920 he taught at Texas Christian University School of Law.

He was hired by the city in 1921 as special counsel in a utility rate case. Three months later he became city attorney.

The 1920s telephone rate case brought him recognition and acclaim. More than 12,000 pages of testimony was generated in the federal court suit. Rouer's brief on behalf of the city ran 1,000 pages.

His thirty-eight years as city attorney were sprinkled with controversy, and the local newspapers covered all of them. In one instance, "failure on a move to oust Rouer resulted in dismissal of a city manager."[12] What politics couldn't achieve, increasing age did. Forced into retirement by a policy requiring city employees to retire at age sixty-eight, he reluctantly switched from municipal to private practice. But by the time of his retirement in 1959, he was acknowledged throughout the nation as an expert in utility rate cases.

On the last day of December 1959, members of the city council spoke eloquently of his many years of service, devotion to the law, skill, loyalty, and integrity. He wasn't there to hear them. Instead he was in court representing the city against giant defense contractor Convair in a tax suit. Later, city fathers, representatives from the legal community, friends, former students, and aides gathered at the posh Fort Worth Club for a luncheon to praise the out-going city attorney. Given a tape of the council meeting, he remarked with typical modesty that having no practice in listening to eulogies about himself, he probably performed a greater service by being in court looking after the city's interests.

His professional and civic activities included membership in the Rotary Club, president of the Tarrant County Bar Association, and vice president of the League of Texas Municipalities. "He was also a member of the House of Delegates of the American Bar Association."[13]

For eight years after his retirement from the city, Rouer was a partner in the firm of Crumley, Rouer, Murphy and Shrull. He died on June 16, 1967, at the age of seventy-six.

Jefferson University School of Law

The end of World War I saw the beginning of the Dallas-based Madison School of Law. For the next ten years the school quietly went about the business of training lawyers. In its 1932 yearbook, *The Jeffersonian*, the editor traced Jefferson University School of Law's origins back to the earlier school. "The Madison College of Law was organized in 1919, for those young men and women who wished to obtain a legal education, but were employed during the day and could not attend classes in a University."[1] Classes were held three nights a week. The curriculum was designed to be covered in three years.

After Madison merged with Jefferson University, also in Dallas, a law school branch was opened in Fort Worth. Organized in 1929 by Andrew J. Priest, LL.D., it initially had three students. "On March 4, 1930, the Supreme Court of Texas signalized the successful efforts of our Faculty," the editor noted, "by placing the School upon its list of approved Law Schools. Ours was thus the fourth school in Texas so recognized."[2]

The Dallas institution moved to new quarters at Harwood and Jackson streets in 1931. Jefferson University had three departments: the School of Commerce and Accounts, the School of Secretarial Training, and the School of Law, which was located in Fort Worth.

Beginning with the fall semester of 1929, classes met in rooms 821-823 of the downtown Fair Building. J. L. Johannes managed the department. Willis M. McGregor, R. V. Nichols, Cecil C. Rotsch, Allan C. Steere, Harry K. Welch, and J. A. Wicks—all practicing attorneys—comprised the faculty.

During the 1931-1932 term, budding lawyers attended lectures by experts in their fields. Carl Chambers began the series with "Necessity of Knowing How to Find the Law." Harry K. Welch followed up with "Principles and Practice of Legal Research." "Practical Hints for the Law Student," was taught by Morris L. Swartsberg. James M. Floyd lectured on taxes. Important to all Texas lawyers was "Oil and Gas Law in Texas," by J. L. Googans.

Arthur S. Haddaway lectured on "Conflict of the Laws." Hal S. Lattimore's topic was "Ethics of the Legal Profession," and Dexter W. Scurlock spoke on the "Code of Ethics of the American Bar."

Four lectures dealt with the nuts and bolts of legal practice. "Libel and Slander" was addressed by Sidney L. Samuels; "Law of Marital Rights in Texas" was taught by the recognized dean of that subject, Ocie Speer. Allan C. Steere lectured on "Operations of Workmen's Compensation Laws." President Andrew J. Priest's discourse was entitled "The Common Law."[3] All the lectures were intended to give students a well-rounded knowledge base.

Ocie Speer wrote the book on marital law.
—Photo courtesy Tarrant County
Bar Association archives

Officers for the 1932 class were T. E. Popplewell, president, David E. Holmes, vice president; Miss Ila Tippitt, secretary; Roger Rhodes, treasurer; and Thomas T. Forbis, sergeant-at-arms.

Gladys Shannon, who lived to be 102 years old, would spend her career after graduation as a probate and income tax lawyer with the firm of Phillips, Trammell, Edwards & Shannon. As a student she wrote in *The Jeffersonian*, the student yearbook, "The Senior Class of 1932 represents a majority of the students who enrolled at the beginning of the school in 1929, when the Fort Worth branch of the Jefferson University was established under the guidance of our good friend, Andrew J. Priest."[4] Editor Shannon explained that only a few fell by the wayside, and a small number of the 1929 class were still working toward graduation. Praised were Ira Butler, George Gleeson, R. C. Cline, B. T. Johnson, and E. C. Pannell for passing the bar after two years at the university.

One of the seniors, a smiling Eva Bloore, was pictured with a pert spitcurl, the style of the period. Thirty years later a picture in the *Fort Worth Star-Telegram* shows a smiling Eva Bloore Barnes, hair still stylish but sprinkled with gray, now the newly elected judge of the Domestic Relations Court Number One of Tarrant County.

Sixteen-year-old Eva's first job, at the magnificent salary of $10.00 a week, was as a typist at the First Baptist Church. A frequent visitor to her boss, Rev. J. Frank Norris, was attorney Chester Collins. Eva's desk was near the entrance to the flamboyant preacher's study, and she made the acquaintance of Collins. His partner, Marvin Simpson, defended Norris in the sensational 1927 trial in which the minister was charged with shooting D. E. Chipps. Collins told Eva to call on him if she ever needed help.

"Things got so bad they were letting several workers go," she recalled.[5] Her choices for employment in 1928 were Woolworth, Montgomery Ward, or the telephone company. She went to see Collins. "Even the building scared me. When I saw that office, all those books, I nearly ran out of there," she remembered with a chuckle.[6] Desperate for a job, she worked for streetcar fare and lunch money. She proved herself and before long earned a salary of $17.50 a week. The diminutive teenager also earned a nickname, "Little Eva," that stuck with her throughout her professional career. Even more importantly, she fell in love—with the law.

Bloore was born in Birmingham, England, but as a small girl came with her parents to Texas. Her father settled in Fort Worth to be near the Southwestern Baptist Theological Seminary. From her mother she learned not to set limits on herself. It was Mrs. Bloore who said, "Eva, you should be a judge."[7] Little did she realize how prophetic her mother was.

When she was nineteen, Bloore read in the newspaper that Jefferson Law School was starting a Fort Worth department. She received little encouragement from her male colleagues, but refused to give up on her dream of making the law her life's work. She went to Dallas and met with the president of Jefferson. Boldly, she offered to open the Fort Worth classroom, keep the books, or help in any other way in exchange for her tuition. President Priest liked the idea of not having to come to Fort Worth several nights a week and took her up on the offer. For three years, three nights a week she went directly from her job in a law office to classes at the law school.

Of her classmates, she remembered there were four women. Both men and women held jobs during the day, and attended the lecture/discussion classes in the evenings.

Bloore and Gladys Shannon passed the bar on their first attempt. Eva was twenty-two, one of the youngest lawyers in the state. But the year was 1932, and new lawyers, both men and women, found jobs scarce. Bloore took a job as a legal secretary. In the mid-1930s she went to New York and worked in a large firm for about a year, but her mother's illness cut short her "big-time" law practice. After her return to Fort Worth she worked first at Cantey and Hanger, then for attorney Arthur Lee Moore as a law clerk.

When Al Clyde returned from World War II, he ran for district attorney in 1945 and won. He offered Bloore, now Eva Barnes, a position as an assistant in his administration. She was ecstatic. Her job with Clyde was her first job as a lawyer, and she was the first female assistant district attorney.

At that time there were few women lawyers, much less working in such a high profile position. Barnes, reflecting on the dif-

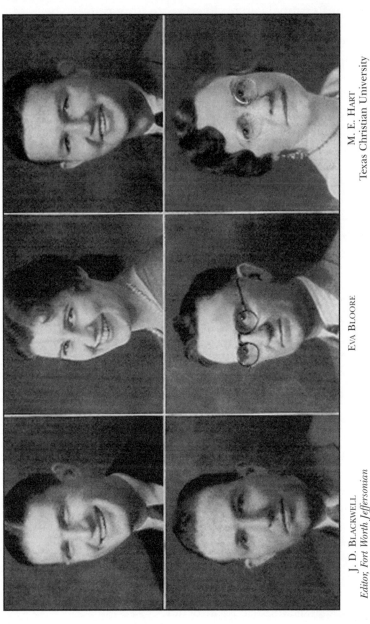

J. D. BLACKWELL
Editor, Fort Worth Jeffersonian
Hobby: Golf

I. A. HART
A. & M. College, C. E.

EVA BLOORE

WILLIAM S. HEAD
Hobby: Baseball

M. E. HART
Texas Christian University
Hobby: Fishing

HELEN HUFF
Hobby: Music

Jefferson University Seniors, 1932.
—Photo courtesy Eva Barnes

R. CURTIS KIMBROUGH
North Texas Teachers College
Hobby: Law

TAYLOR M. MCCLELLAND
Hobby: Golf

J. FRANK ROBERTS
Texas Christian University

LA VERNE RODMAN
Texas Christian University

GLADYS SHANNON
North Texas Teachers College
Hobby: Swimming

D. E. WALSH
Texas Military School
Hobby: Military Activities

V. D. WILSON
Hobby: Sightseeing

Jefferson University Seniors, 1932.
—Photo courtesy Eva Barnes

ficulty of working in a "man's world" said, "I have always tried to keep from feeling that some men were prejudiced against me in any way."[8] Instead, she used friendship and respect toward male colleagues, and it was reciprocated.

After Clyde left the district attorney's office, the two went into private practice. One of their cases was defending Arthur C. Hester. In the much publicized 1949 trial, the eighteen-year-old was accused of murdering Texas Christian University professor Dr. John Lord. Barnes made her first full-fledged jury speech, one which had courtroom spectators in tears. It was broadcast over a statewide radio hookup. Another first. They lost the case, but she gained recognition as an able trial lawyer.

Long interested in politics, in the 1930s she served as secretary of the "Young Democrats." She was one of twenty Fort Worth people invited to meet with President Franklin D. Roosevelt in his private railroad car when he stopped in Wichita Falls—a meeting she recalled as the greatest excitement of her young life. When W. Lee O'Daniel ran for governor in 1938, Jesse Martin, Eva's boss, worked in his campaign, which meant that she indirectly worked in it.

Years later, supported by her husband, Marvin Barnes, it seemed only natural for Eva to extend her love of the law to the bench. She ran for office in 1962 and racked up another first. Although women had been appointed to the bench, she was the first woman elected on her own merits.

Dressed in a royal blue Chanel style suit with matching pillbox hat, she took the oath of office from Judge Leo Brewster. "I feel that I am qualified in every respect to handle the important matters that will come before such a court," she told reporters.[9]

Judge Barnes followed a schedule of hearing juvenile cases on Mondays, and divorce cases Wednesday through Friday. "Tuesday is her headache day, the day her court is filled with fathers in contempt for not paying child support."[10] That also was the day her bailiff always formally announced, "All rise," when she entered. She wanted everyone to realize they were in court on a serious charge.

Eva was so well-liked in the legal community that lawyers needed to remember to refer to her as Judge Barnes. "After all, it wouldn't be very dignified for a lawyer, engaged in a heated argument, to stand up in court and say to the judge: 'Now, Little Eva.'"[11] Judge "Little Eva" was re-elected four times before her retirement in 1979.

As an assistant district attorney she spearheaded a move to re-word portions of the Texas adoption laws. Her years on the bench were peppered with tragic cases in which children were emotionally harmed by combative divorcing parents or absent parents. She worked tirelessly for children's welfare and the betterment of their situations.

Upon her retirement, friends and colleagues presented her with a thick scrapbook filled with letters of praise and momentos. Juvenile Judge Lynn Ross wrote, "I believe she had the longest, most continuous interest in children of any person I ever worked with."[12] The scrapbook weighed almost as much as the gracious lady they honored.

Bloore's fellow student George Patrick Gleeson began his study of law at the old Madison College of Law and received his degree from Jefferson. Like Bloore, he had little cash and bartered for his law school education. Prior to his legal career he was owner of radio station KFQB, the forerunner of KFJZ. He gave free advertising to the school in exchange for tuition. "I remember my father coming home from the radio station at midnight and studying until dawn," recalled George P. Gleeson, Jr.[13]

His diploma reads, "To all to whom these presents may come, greeting: know ye, that George P. Gleeson having completed the course of Legal Study . . . now, therefore, we do confer upon him the Degree of Bachelor of Law." It is signed by Andrew J. Priest, president. He was admitted to the Bar in September 1931 and ". . . is authorized to practice as an attorney and counselor at law in all the Courts of the State of Texas."[14] He practiced in Fort Worth until 1943.

Gleeson served in the Merchant Marine Corps from 1943 until 1947. While in the service he helped organize USO centers in Australia, the Panama Canal Zone, and the Philippine Islands.

Back in civilian life, he resumed his law practice. Gleeson was elected to the American Bar Association and became a member of the Commercial Law League of America in 1947.

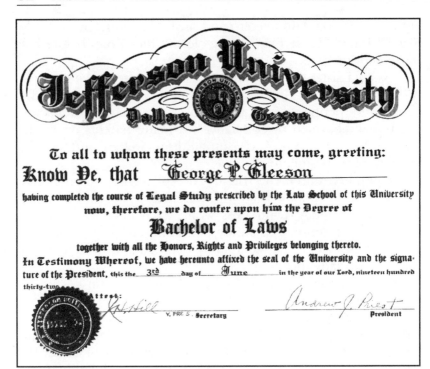

George Gleeson, Sr.'s Law School Diploma.
—Courtesy George Gleeson, Jr.

The following year he was admitted to practice before the Interstate Commerce Commission. Gleeson specialized in helping to organize and incorporate municipalities. In that capacity he was instrumental in directing the incorporation of Colleyville, Everman, Euless, Forest Hill, Haltom City, River Oaks, Southlake, Westlake, Westworth Village, and White Settlement.

A member of St. Patrick's Cathedral, he participated actively in the Knights of Columbus. He also served on the board of directors of St. Teresa's Home. Gleeson loved the Shrine Circus and took pride in the fact that his silk hat, part of the Knights regalia, was for years used by the ringmaster of the circus.

His life and career were captured in Senate Resolution No. 296, in memory of Mr. George Patrick Gleeson. It reads:

Whereas, In the passing of George Patrick Gleeson of Fort Worth and Tarrant County, Texas, on 4 February, 1960, the people of Texas lost a beloved citizen and distinguished lawyer;

Whereas, George was an expert in municipal law and served as counselor to numerous cities in Texas. He was a scholar and student and gave of his time freely to young lawyers who needed advice in his specialized field of the law; and

Whereas, Although too old for military service in World War II, he volunteered for service four years in the United States Merchant Marines, helping transport cargoes to all sections of the globe to sustain the efforts of American youth fighting in these areas for our democratic ideals; and ...

Resolved, That copies of this Memorial Resolution be sent to his family with the deep regard of the Texas Senate. Signed by Ben Ramsey, President of the Senate.[15]

Other notable graduates of the Jefferson School of Law included David E. Holmes, Arthur A. Diehl, and David P. Netterville.

Holmes graduated from Thorp Springs Christian College in 1925. While working in Fort Worth he attended night classes at Jefferson. An article in the *Texas Bar Journal* stated, "Even as a boy on his father's farm, young Holmes dreamed of becoming a lawyer, and induced his brother, E. G. Holmes, Jr. to study law."[16] His legal career was spent as an investigator with the Retail Credit Company, Inc. following his 1932 admission to the bar. The Granbury native died at the age of thirty-six after a long illness.

The other David in the class, Netterville, specialized in real estate. The Mississippi native was associated with Stewart Title Company for forty-four years before his 1963 retirement.

The 1932 senior class contained four women. In addition to the three already mentioned was Helen Huff. Huff was admitted to the bar in 1933 and worked for the Fort Worth and Denver Railroad. Like classmate Gleeson, she was licensed to practice before the Interstate Commerce Commission. "Miss Huff organized the Woman's Traffic Club of Fort Worth, the first such club formed in Texas, and she served as its president," according to the *Star-Telegram.*[17]

Jefferson University's junior and freshman classes (being a three-year school, there was no sophomore class) were all male.

The yearbook contained this assessment of the growing wisdom to freshmen:

> The law student in his first year when asked the law, on a certain state of facts, answers, "The law is this."
>
> The same student in his second year when asked the same question will answer, "I think the law is this."
>
> The same student in his senior year when asked the same question will answer, "Judge, wait until I can go look up the law."[18]
>
> In the year to come, we the student body, hope to be able to look upon the old ALMA MATER, as a University, second to none, for those young men and women who wish to attain higher learning.[19]

Unfortunately, it was not to be. The school was re-chartered in 1933 as the North Texas School of Law.

The North Texas
School of Law

Fragile, retired attorney Tom Murphy, Jr., amid a lifetime of memorabilia, treasures his framed diploma. It reads:

> This certifies that Thomas Joseph Murphy, Jr. having completed the course of study prescribed by the Faculty, and having complied with all requirements for the issuance of the Degree herein conferred, is now honorably graduated from the North Texas School of Law, and is hereby awarded the Degree of Bachelor of Laws, and is entitled to all the rights and appurtenances thereof.
>
> In Witness Whereof, The members of the Faculty have hereunto affixed their signatures at Fort Worth, Texas, this 23 day of May, A.D. 1941.[1]

It is signed by H. K. Welch, S. A. Crowley, E. E. Sanders, George L. Rice, R.V. Nichols, and Juliet M. Sedbury.

More than fifty years later Murphy reminisced about his law school experiences. "Tuition was $35.00 a semester."[2] He noted it had been higher, and indeed at one time the tuition was $45.00 for three courses. The men, there were no women students as he recalled, met in a large room at 108½ E. Ninth Street. The school rented space from the Southern Business College. There were "about twenty-five attending classes" in the years he was there.[3] All worked during the day and went to class at night.

Asked about taking the bar examination, he replied, "I remember that distinctly. We had four written exams a day; two in the morning and two in the afternoon."[4] He and fellow aspirants studied until 2:00 A.M. for the sixteen-part examination. Murphy explained that those who failed could take the examination as many as three times. He passed, and was notified by mail. His alma mater boasted, "The record of graduates of this school surpasses the showing made by graduates of many full time Universities."[5]

Most of Murphy's career was spent working for oil companies. After graduation he signed on with Texaco, first in their Fort Worth office, then transferred to Midland. In 1955 he became an independent land man, researching abstracts and deeds for several corporations. His work took him to East and South Texas and New Mexico, but the bulk of his operation was in West Texas.

Harry K. Welch, whom Murphy remembered as being a friendly and capable instructor, "ramrodded the law school."[6] Officially organized in June 1933, the goal of the North Texas School of Law was to provide an opportunity for students to equip themselves for the legal profession while pursuing their livelihood. Welch, S. A. Crowley, and George W. Rice were listed on the incorporation papers. Welch had been a professor at the now defunct Jefferson School of Law and eased the transition between the two schools.

"The North Texas School of Law offers a three year course of study leading to the degree of Bachelor of Laws."[7] Subjects included were agency, bailments and carriers, civil procedure, common law, constitutional law, contracts, criminal law, domestic relations, evidence, Federal procedure, torts, and wills and estates. The Case Book method, the same system used at Yale, Harvard, the University of Texas, and other leading law schools, gave students actual reported cases to study.

Classes met Monday, Wednesday, and Friday nights from 6:30 to 8:30. On Wednesdays after classes, moot court sessions were held until 10:30. "At each session several of the students, assisted by the instructors, act as lawyers in a trial that is conducted essentially like a real case."[8] Each year's work was divided into two semesters of four-and-one-half months each. Students were able to complete six courses a year, finishing the program in three years.

In 1935 the enrollment was forty-five. Tom Murphy noted that when jobs were hard to find men took classes to enhance their ability to get a job or be promoted in one already held. His observation seems on target as enrollment dropped when the economy began to improve in the late 1930s.

The faculty was composed of graduates of the leading law universities of the Southwest. All were practicing attorneys, and besides teaching the theory of the law, were able to impart to students a working knowledge of court procedure. This dual expertise, according to one graduate, guaranteed the best possible legal education.

The much-revered Welch was born in Decatur, but attended Paschal High School. He earned the LL.B. degree from the University of Texas in 1925. From that time until his death in 1971, he spent his entire career in Fort Worth. After passing the bar, he was associated with Ross Title Insurance Company. In 1929 Welch became director and vice-president of Union Title and Trust Company. Three years later he and Carl M. Johnson purchased the company and re-named it the Fort Worth and Tarrant County Abstract Company.

Welch taught for eight years at the law school he helped establish. Attorney J. Olcott Phillips described Welch as a brilliant man and skilled professor. When not in the classroom or office, he could be found on the golf course or at his ranch south of the city.

Seymour native Robert Vernon Nichols was another important leader at the school. He served as president and dean in addition to his teaching duties. Nichols, a Baptist, graduated from Baylor University College of Law in 1928. That same year he passed the bar and began his career in Fort Worth.

The 1948 political scene was testy and Nichols, Democratic chairman of Precinct 107, made the news when he protested the need to sign a loyalty oath. "I have never supported the Republican Party, the Texas Regulars, the Dixiecrats or any other political party during the years of my voting life and never

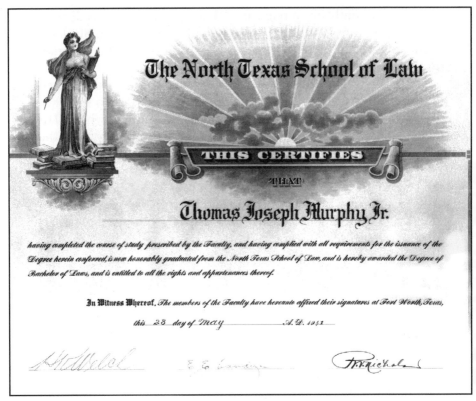

*Robert V. Nichols signed Thomas J. Murphy, Jr.'s diploma
from North Texas School of Law.*
—Photo courtesy of Thomas J. Murphy, Jr.

intend to," he said.[9] He reluctantly signed, feeling he had an obligation to those who voted for him. At the time of his protest Nichols was the newly elected president of the Tarrant County Bar Association.

He was active in the state bar, serving as a director of the Twelfth Congressional District. Bennett Smith wrote of Nichols, "He was on the board of directors from 1951 to 1954 and was a member of the State Bar Committee on Modifications in the Organization of the Bar, and Committees on Bar Admission, Budget, Legal Education, Legal Aid and Unauthorized Practice of Law."[10] Nichols, speaking as chairman of the Downtown Kiwanis Club's public affairs committee, suggested to the 1951 grand jury investigating vice in the county that a "citizens' crime commission could be healthy here."[11] He stressed he had no political motive, but wanted to acquaint the jury with the successful efforts of such commissions in other cities.

He also served on the Tarrant County Crime Commission and the board of directors of the Fort Worth Area Chamber of Commerce.

Nichols, a World War II veteran, was active in the American Legion, and a member of the Selective Service Board for a quarter of a century. A deacon and Sunday School teacher at Broadway Baptist Church, he died in 1974 at the age of sixty-six.

Robert V. Nichols, dean and president of North Texas School of Law.
—Photo courtesy of Robert B. Nichols

Tom Murphy remembered Nichols' colleague, George W. Rice, as a physically imposing man, but with a gentle spirit. He maintained offices in the Capps Building with Bryant K. Goree. He later joined Welch as vice president of Fort Worth and Tarrant County Abstract Company.

J. Everette Cline was one of three brothers, all lawyers. In addition to teaching at the North Texas School of Law, and practicing law, he was active in civic affairs. He served as president of the North Side Kiwanis Club in 1939 and four years later took the gavel of the Fort Worth Bar Association.

J. Olcott Phillips remembered Cline as a very capable instructor who specialized in civil cases. Phillips, who graduated in 1940, regarded his education at the North Texas School of Law as the best of all worlds. Teachers and students shared a mutual respect because of the two-pronged emphasis on theory and practical application. Professors were experts in their areas of specialization because they were actively practicing law while teaching it. Often students, such as Phillips, worked in law offices and were familiar with the latest case law to be covered in class discussions. "There were no restraints about asking questions and the intellectual give and take was stimulating for both students and professors," he recalled.[12] Phillips was only one of several of the school's graduates who enjoyed distinguished careers in the practice of law.

Herbert J. Brown, a classmate of Phillips, was an engineer as well as an attorney. He held certificates in jig and fixture design and in engineering, science, and management defense training from Texas A&M University. In writing of Brown, historian Smith noted, "While attending law school at night, he taught mechanical drafting at Technical High School in Fort Worth."[13]

After passing the bar Brown worked in the tool design and patent department of Convair, now Lockheed Martin. In addition to his Texas credentials, he was licensed to practice before the Supreme Court, the U.S. Court of Customs and Patent Appeals, the U.S. Court of Claims, and the Fifth Circuit Court of Appeals in New Orleans.

His interest in patents led to an article, "Patent Information for the General Practitioner" which appeared in the *Texas Bar Journal*. Another issue of that journal told of Brown's wide range of interests. "He had also written and produced color films with accompanying commentaries entitled '19 Patents Which Changed the World.'"[14] A devout churchman, Brown also wrote essays on "Early Days of Westcliff Methodist Church," "Christian Symbols," and "Stars and Planets." In a paper, "The World We Live In," he covered the Creation to the end of Creation as he interpreted it based on his scientific research and Bible study.

In addition to his engineering and writing skills, he was musically talented. Brown entertained family and close friends by playing his console organ. He suffered a fatal heart attack in 1971 at age sixty-one.

Code E. Edwards was a lawyer who became a war hero. He graduated in 1937 with the LL.B. degree from North Texas School of Law. Edwards worked for the Internal Revenue Service until the outbreak of World War II. A member of the Army Signal Corps, he saw action in the Southern Philippine campaigns. The *Texas Bar Journal* extolled his military record by stating, "He received the Asiatic-Pacific Campaign medal with two bronze stars, the Philippine Liberation Ribbon, the American Theatre Campaign Medal and the Victory Medal."[15]

After the war, he returned to Fort Worth and joined the firm of Gilbert, Edwards & Colvin as a specialist in estate and tax law. Following his death in 1974, President Gerald Ford presented the family a memorial citation, lauding Edwards' "devoted and selfless consecration to the service of our country."[16]

Joe Shannon, Sr. was another decorated World War II hero who received his professional training at the North Texas School of Law. His military exploits, according to the *Star-Telegram*, were as a tailgunner on B-17 bombers. As a result of his thirty-two missions over Europe, Shannon was awarded the Air Medal with three Oak Leaf Clusters and the Distinguished Flying Cross. "He participated in missions over Berlin and Normandy during D-Day. On one occasion, he was on a mission that dropped supplies to the underground in Warsaw, Poland, and went on to land in Russia before returning to England."[17]

After the war, proudly wearing his "ruptured duck" discharge lapel pin, he became an assistant district attorney. He resigned that post when he was elected with a more than 10,000 vote majority to the Texas Legislature in 1948. Shannon served his Tarrant and Denton County constituents for two terms.

To his good fortune, Shannon's interest in law preceded his interest in politics. "He attended old Central High School, where he met his future wife during a mock trial in which she was the court reporter and he was 'defense attorney.' They were married in 1938."[18]

When not in Austin, Shannon practiced with Otis Rogers and Joe Spurlock, Sr. In 1952 he resumed his private practice full-time. Shannon died in 1975, after three influential decades as a member of the legal community. His legacy is being carried on by Joe Shannon, Jr., LL.B.

Another lawyer family was that of Robert Coleman Cline. The McKinney native attended North Fort Worth High School, the University of Texas, and Texas Christian University before graduating from the North Texas School of Law. After admission to the bar, he joined his brothers W. Alvis and J. Everett in the firm of Cline & Cline. J. Everett was also an instructor at the law school. Robert's memberships included local and state bar associations and Boulevard United Methodist Church. He died in June 1975 at the age of seventy-four.

North Texas graduate and oil specialist Curtis Kimbrough began his work with Gulf Oil Corporation in 1927. He was one of those who chose to go to law school to increase his skills. Admitted to the bar in 1934, he remained with Gulf for the next twenty years. In 1954 Kimbrough opened an office in the new Fair East Shopping Center on East Lancaster. Civic activities included director of the Y.M.C.A., membership in the Polytechnic Chapter of Royal Arch Mason Lodge, and president and chanter of the Shrine. Active in the Polytechnic Presbyterian Church, he at one time or another held almost all church offices except pastor.

Businessman William O. Freeman began his law studies about the time Kimbrough finished his. Freeman received a B.A. degree from Texas Christian University in 1923, and served as personnel director for Armour and Company for seventeen years. He was admitted to the Texas Bar in 1938 and became a senior member of the Freeman & War firm. His interests were wide-ranging. He was a member of the Fort Worth Library Board, past president of the Fort Worth Farm and Ranch Club, and past officer of the Palomino Association. In addition to palomino horses, he raised Angus cattle when not writing legal briefs.

Classmate Landrum Edward Weeden specialized in tax law. He passed the bar in 1939, and was engaged in the practice of tax law in the North Texas area serving the cities of Commerce and Brazoria, and the counties of El Paso, Henderson, and Tarrant.

He was a native of Lone Oak, where he attended public school. Later he studied at Burleson College and North Texas State College before attending law school.

One of the later graduates was Robert G. Berryman. He received a law degree in 1940. His legal career was spent as counsel to the air force at General Dynamics. He was a Fort Worth resident for fifty years prior to his death in 1975.

Many of the graduates of the North Texas School of Law served in the armed forces or civilian jobs related to the war effort. J. Olcott Phillips finished his course work, took the bar exam, and received notice he had passed after he was in the army. Other young men who would have started law school instead were in the service. This lack of students, much like the problem faced by Texas Christian University during World War I, was a main factor in the disbanding of the school. Once again North Texans who desired a law degree were forced to leave the area or go to Dallas for day classes at Southern Methodist University.

The Dallas/Fort Worth Law School

Robert L. "Bob" Harmon is the type of person who, when he sees a need, does something about it. He saw a need for a night law school in the Dallas-Fort Worth area and started one. The original name chosen was North Texas School of Law, but the University of North Texas in nearby Denton objected, claiming the name would cause people to confuse it with their institution. Whatever the name, for Harmon the need for a night school was personal. In the early 1960s he wanted to study law in the metroplex, but Southern Methodist University Law School had discontinued its night classes. He went elsewhere.

Twenty-five years later he formed an *ad hoc* committee to do a feasibility study to see if a night law school was viable. The committee polled area pre-law students and found great interest in the idea. With the help of Randy Robinson, Alan Smith, and the late Steve Chaney, the Dallas/Fort Worth School of Law, a non-profit corporation, was a reality.

Cofounder Steve Chaney grew up in East Fort Worth, and was one of the first to graduate from the new Eastern Hills High School. After getting his law degree from the University of Texas, he was a military judge in the Marine Corps for four years. He returned to his home city and joined the firm of Shannon and Shannon. When Tim Curry was elected district attorney, Chaney became an assistant. At the time of his death he was senior staff attorney in Curry's office.

"He loved the law, and believed the Dallas/Fort Worth Law School would be a way to promote the teaching of legal ethics, a subject of keen interest to him." his widow recalled.[1]

Chaney's vision was to establish a school in downtown Fort Worth, as close to the courthouse as possible. He shared Harmon's determination to provide metroplex men and women the opportunity to get a law degree without leaving the area or giving up their livelihoods.

The Dallas/Fort Worth Law School opened in August 1989 with Harmon as president and CEO. *Fort Worth Star-Telegram* reporter Linda Campbell noted that "the school offers the only night law school classes between Waco and Oklahoma City."[2]

Assistant District Attorney Steve Chaney helped get Dallas/Fort Worth Law School established.
—Photo courtesy Steve Chaney family

Harmon *et al.* first leased classroom space from the University of Dallas, a Catholic institution. Dallas/Fort Worth Law School started with a large classroom and two offices in what had been a convent. One student remembered the setting as quaint and unique, but adequate. A library was bought from Garza University in South Texas, but the books arrived before the school had space for them. Harmon stored the books in commercial storage facilities until room was found to shelve them.

The fledgling faculty consisted of John Cady, Sue Pertil, and Joe Spurlock II. Later Frank Elliott came on as dean, and Steve Alton, Robert Gray, Malinda Seymore, and Shirley Zaebel taught there.

In the admission process, the faculty studied prospective students' grade point averages and Law School Admission Test scores. That first year faculty personally interviewed applicants. Work or life experiences that gave an indication of a student's chances of succeeding were also considered. The 104 beginning students took four basic courses, with each class meeting twice weekly, Monday through Thursday.

John Cady taught torts; Frank Elliott, civil procedure; Sue Pertil, contracts; and Joe Spurlock II, still judge of the Court of Appeals at the time, taught research and writing. At the end of the first year, eighty-two students made history as the initial class of Dallas/Fort Worth Law School.

Part of the convent housed a girls' school. This combination made for an interesting mix; giggling girls running up and down the halls with adults, tired after working all day, trying to absorb serious legal material. In its second year of operation the school was promised more space to house the growing enrollment. But with space not forthcoming, and the incompatibility of a law school and a girls' school under one roof, Harmon decided to seek another location. With

Frank Elliott, dean of Dallas/Fort Worth Law School.
—Photo courtesy of Texas Wesleyan University

the help of Texas Appeals Court Justice Ed Kinkeade, they found one in the Recognition Equipment Company computer center on Grauwyler Road in Irving. When the school moved to the new, bigger quarters, "We considered taping the noise and playing it during classes so everyone would feel at home," Harmon mused.[3]

The student body at Dallas/Fort Worth Law School consisted of men and women who had a strong commitment to persevere and graduate with a law degree. They juggled family, work, and school, intent on achieving their goal. Because they were more mature and determined than younger, "traditional" students, they developed a camaraderie not found in larger schools. Not only did they help each other, they helped the school. When the American Bar Association cited the school for not having an adequate library, students each took a state and subscribed to its bar journal for all to use.

They helped in other ways as well. Attorney Nancy Berger recalled, "When the pipes above the library leaked, we moved the books to a dry area."[4] Berger, who graduated in 1994 after the school merged with Texas Wesleyan, felt she and others got a good education, thanks to hard work and the guidance of their excellent instructors.

After two years of operation, Dallas/Fort Worth Law School proved without a doubt a night school could succeed. Professor Elliott, recalling the early days, said, "We knew that it was very difficult for a stand alone law school to get accredited, not impossible, but it would be easier if we were under a university umbrella."[5]

The board of trustees looked around for someone with whom they could merge and grow. The University of Dallas and Texas Christian University were considered, but those schools had other priorities. Harmon, a Texas Wesleyan alumnus, first talked with Texas Wesleyan University President Jerry Baucom. He embraced the possibility, but left to become president at the University of Mary Hardin-Baylor. Incoming Wesleyan President Jake Schrum was even more receptive to the idea. Serious discussions were held for a year.

Wesleyan board trustee Gary Cumbie, reflecting on the Wesleyan board's deliberations prior to the merger, indicated their enthusiasm was tempered with caution. Three factors were thoroughly weighed. The first was that it was important to the board that the Dallas/Fort Worth school and Wesleyan share parallel philosophies concerning serving the needs of the community. As they studied the matter, it became apparent that a night law school fit Wesleyan's goal of becoming a leader in the "Urban University" concept of higher education. To that end Wesleyan already had plans for what would become the C. E. Hyde Weekend University for full-time employed students. The possible synergy of the two schools excited Wesleyan trustees enough to further explore the proposal.

The second factor trustees considered was the support of the business and legal community. That wariness was laid to rest when Ken Devero, president of "Downtown Fort Worth, Inc." gave the university his organization's support. "The law school's move downtown would be 'outstanding.'"[6] Devero also noted it would fit in nicely with the strategic action plan for downtown, which called for an education center and one or more professional schools.

The third and perhaps most critical element was money. "We knew it would cost a lot of money and we didn't want to cripple the main campus," Cumbie said.[7] The question they asked themselves was could they afford a law school, or would it be better to spend the money elsewhere? "When we looked at it, not only did the law school's mission fit, but it gave us the ability to really become a university."[8]

Dallas/Fort Worth Law School, Inc. President Harmon, in July 1992, sold the school to Texas Wesleyan for a nominal sum and joined the university as a vice president to ease the transition. From Wesleyan's point of view it helped that a faculty and curriculum were already in place. The professors embraced the likelihood of greater stability under the umbrella of an established university. "Joining the old Dallas/Fort Worth School of Law to Texas Wesleyan University certainly was the best thing to happen to both the law school and the university in recent memory," according to the *Business Press*.[9] The Dallas/Fort Worth Law School enjoyed a short but very important history. The founders saw a need and acted.

Texas Wesleyan University School of Law

A centennial brochure proclaims, "Texas Wesleyan University, founded in 1890 . . . is a United Methodist institution with a tradition of integrating the liberal arts and sciences with professional and career preparation at the undergraduate level and in selected graduate areas."[1] A committee of Methodists, led by founder Bishop Joseph S. Key, explored sites for a campus, and settled on land east of Fort Worth donated by A. S. Hall, W. D. Hall, and George Tandy. Originally called Polytechnic College, the September 1891 class was composed of 111 students.

Since the beginning, Wesleyan has combined service to a traditional on-campus student body with a strong desire to accommodate its commuting and adult population. And so, some one hundred years after its founding, Texas Wesleyan University added a school of law. Two years later, "To add flexibility in the scheduling of courses and recognize the special needs of adult learners, the University added the C. E. Hyde Weekend University in 1994."[2] President Jake Schrum, speaking to a group of university presidents from across the country, addressed the growing diversity of today's students. The theme of the Sundance Symposium conference in Fort Worth was to explain the meaning and mission of the "New Urban University."

"The 'New Urban University' is simply a way of explaining what we've been doing for more than 100 years," Schrum told the assembled educators.[3] He went on to say, "That means making education more accessible to the mainstream of America by giving students the kind of education they need at a time and a place that makes a university education possible."[4] A North Texas night law school was part of meeting that need.

Texas Wesleyan University's board of trustees voted unanimously on July 21, 1992, to buy the Dallas/Fort Worth School of Law and bring it to Fort Worth. If one considered only the cash outlay, it was the bargain of the century. "President Jake Schrum said the university will acquire the law school for 'ten dollars and all the valuable considerations.'"[5] On August 1 the official name became the Texas Wesleyan University School of Law. The move was seen as advantageous for both. Wesleyan would strengthen its undergraduate pre-law program and

Frank K. Walwer, professor and dean, Texas Wesleyan School of Law.

—Photo courtesy of TWU School of Law

Dallas/Fort Worth students could expect to graduate from an accredited school.

In 1994 Frank K. Walwer took the reins as dean. A man of wide experience, the Columbia University graduate had been associate dean at his alma mater, and dean of the University of Tulsa College of Law. Walwer's professional activities included membership on the American Bar Association accreditation committee. Clearly, Texas Wesleyan University trustees believed he was the man who would know how to get the school fully

President Jake Schrum signs papers to buy the 1515 Commerce location for the law school.

—Photo courtesy Texas Wesleyan University School of Law

accredited. "I'm not here just as a matter of accreditation. . . . If the ABA finds things of concern, then we'll fix them. Instead, we're concentrating on the elements of the law center," he said.[6]

For the first five years the school of law remained in rented quarters in Irving. One of Dean Elliott's initial tasks was to find a permanent home for the school, as the American Bar Association would not extend accreditation without it. President Schrum resolved it should be in a very visible, downtown location. After scouting several available sites, 1515 Commerce Street was selected. Of modern design, the tan stucco building, formerly owned by Southwestern Bell Telephone Company, sits across the street from the city's scenic Water Gardens.

On November 4, 1996, Gregg Upp, representing the telephone company, figuratively gave the keys to President Schrum, along with the current tenant, a branch office of the Internal Revenue Service. "The tax-collector jokes were almost as inevitable as, well, taxes," reporter Linda Campbell quipped.[7] Louis Sturns, president of the Tarrant County Bar Association, noted it was nice to be in the building without being audited. During the opening celebration puzzled taxpayers, there for audits, ducked in and out of elevators, wondering what all the hoopla was about. In *The Rambler*, the Texas Wesleyan student newspaper, the lead story proclaimed, "The Texas Wesleyan law school moved closer to full accreditation and to the main campus after President Jake Schrum signed closing papers on the purchase of the former Southwestern Bell building Monday."[8]

A $2.8 million loan from Texas Commerce Bank provided funds for both the property and money for renovation.

With the location problem settled, Dean Walwer focused his attention on accreditation. The ABA had visited the Irving campus in 1991 and withheld approval for provisional status. Three years later it was a different story. In April the inspection committee toured the improved facility and interviewed professors and students. They found that Wesleyan had added more than 2,000 books to the library, and enlarged the faculty and staff. These changes, plus the commitment to move, led the committee to recommend provisional accreditation. In a voice vote at its House of Delegates meeting in New Orleans the recommendation was accepted. Bill Teeter of the *Star-Telegram* reported,

"Gaining provisional accreditation was vital for the law school. . . . Without [it], the law school's graduates would not be allowed to take the state bar examination or practice law in Texas and some other states."[9] President Schrum welcomed the news and vowed to continue pressing until the next step, total accredition, would be granted.

The elation over the ABA action was not shared by the discovery that those who finished their course work would be required to graduate before the effective accreditation date. Those students believed this was contrary to an agreement between themselves and the school. Being lawyers, they sued. "The students really want to make a point. They don't want to make money off this. They really just want to have a degree from an accredited school," said Susan Mayfield, their attorney.[10] After approval of the American Bar Association and the Texas Supreme Court, the suit was settled with the students getting appropriately dated diplomas and Wesleyan paying attorneys fees and court costs. Lawyer R. Brent Cooper acknowledged "the students believed that the school had intended all along to let them graduate after accreditation was granted but that it was prevented from doing so 'because of intimidation by the ABA.'"[11] Relations were somewhat strained, but Dean Walwer said the school was pleased with the outcome. "We very much look forward to working with all our alumni in the ongoing development and program of the Texas Wesleyan Law School," he said. "We are gratified to have the matter behind us."[12]

With two major hurdles behind him, Dean Walwer concentrated on getting the Commerce Street property ready for occupancy while running a growing law school. The move itself, carried out over a weekend, was well planned and orderly.

Professor Frank Elliott said a couple of his pictures got routed to someone else's office, but there were no big problems. Elliott, whose office is decorated in a western theme, sports a cowhide area rug and other Old West memorabilia, including the wayward pictures and a wall of certificates and recognitions.

Saturday, November 15, 1997, dawned cold and windy. Scattered patches of snow clung to the grass as a band of hardy supporters gathered for the Texas Wesleyan University School of Law dedication. Sidney Roberts, secretary to the board of

Fort Worth Mayor Kenneth Barr, President Jake Schrum, and Congresswoman Kay Granger, and other dignitaries at the dedication of the Texas Wesleyan University School of Law.

—Photo courtesy TWU School of Law

trustees, delivered the invocation. Greetings were brought by Jake B. Schrum; Loren Q. Hanson, chairman of the board of trustees; and Wade H. McMullen, president-elect of the Tarrant County Bar Association. Dean Frank K. Walwer gave a brief history of the school, and James M. Bridge, president of the Student Bar Association spoke for his class. Provost Thomas F. Armstrong, a historian, spoke on the development of legal education.

Wesleyan alumna U.S. Representative Kay Granger and

Fort Worth Mayor Kenneth Barr cut the blue and gold ribbon and ushered guests into the sparkling facility.

Wesleyan had renovated the two lower floors to house classrooms, administration and faculty offices, and a practice courtroom that could be walled off into a classroom.

The use of glass partitions and greenery gives the facility a feeling of openness. The subtle mélange of colors in the carpeting soothes the eye and provides warmth. In addition to regular classrooms, tiered seating in two large auditoriums provides easy visibility for all. Modern electronic teaching/learning aids are seen throughout the building. The Fall 1997 class, first to use the new quarters, "oohed and aahed over their new digs," reporter Campbell wrote.[13]

The law library comprises a large part of the lower floor. The *Programs, Policies & Procedures* booklet for 1998-1999 states, "The primary mission of the Texas Wesleyan University Law Library is to provide access to the legal information sources needed for student course work and research."[14] That information is in the form of books containing case decisions, on-line electronic legal information services, law journals, and newspapers. U.S. congressional documents on microfiche include full transcripts of all congressional hearings since 1970. "In addition to on-line services, the Law Library subscribes to several sources of law published in CD-ROM format."[15] According to James Hambleton, executive director of Texas Wesleyan's Law Library, "The American Bar Association is now looking at the total ability to provide legal information rather than simply the number of books in a library. Title count is a more appropriate way to judge the worth of a law library."[16] Thanks to the internet, he noted during the school's dedication, "a judge's order posted on the Worldwide Web can be viewed in Lubbock at the same time as in London."[17]

Hambleton sees two important changes in the modern law library. One, students can now work at home, via computer, as well as do research in the library proper; and secondly, the graphic representation has been greatly improved. He went on to say at one time computer generated legal information looked like any other narrative printout. Now, thanks to specialized software, a court case is in a format comparable to a court reporter's authentic document.

In addition to the expanded use of electronic technology, which Hambleton stresses will only increase, he views open access of the library as an important way to fulfill Wesleyan's mission of serving the community. "The Law Library is open more than 110 hours per week, during 85 of which a professional law librarian is on duty."[18] Practicing attorneys and the general public are welcomed, and since the library is open until midnight week-days, many down-

Law Library Director James Hambleton helps a student.
—Photo courtesy of TWU School of Law

town workers use it after they get off work. Five study rooms are available for use by two or more students for group study or discussion.

The "Law Library Guide" lists as available, "The Microfiche Reading room contains microfilm and microfiche of U.S. treaties, law reviews, the Congressional Record, the Congressional Information Service and Serial Set, the Federal Register, Code of Federal Regulations, United States Reports, Federal Cases, Uniform State Laws, American Law Institute Proceedings, SEC Decisions and Reports, Federal Trade Commission reports, Federal Power Commission Reports, U.S. Decisions of the Comptroller General, Texas session laws, Vernon's Annotated

Texas Statutes (Civil), Texas constitutional Conventions, Texas Register, and Texas Attorney General materials."[19]

Because Texas Wesleyan University School of Law focuses on graduating practitioners rather than researchers, the library has an extensive collection of Texas law books, and those of contiguous states, but less materials of a national or international nature beyond those listed above.

The student lounge features comfortable blue plastic and chrome chairs and round beige topped tables, vending machines, and bulletin and message boards. Racks holding *The Rambler, Fort Worth Weekly*, and other newspapers are available to read while eating a snack. Along one wall are hanging folders, one for each student. The blue mail and message folders, arranged alphabetically, are for Level I students, the olive folders are for upper level classmates. Lockers provide storage space for students' books and backpacks. On a whimsical note, a yellow gum ball machine, filled with multicolored "jaw breakers," stands ready to dispense its goodies to anyone with twenty-five cents.

In its new location the school has prospered. A 1997-1998 Fact Sheet published by Wesleyan shows an enrollment of 376 full-time and 282 part-time students of which approximately forty per cent are women and twenty-one per cent are minorities. Asked what women bring to the legal community, Associate Dean Malinda L. Seymore cited such important trends as the recognition of women's issues as legitimate areas of study and the different viewpoints that women offer, especially related to mediation law.

"The student body's diversity can be seen in the 81 undergraduate institutions represented in the 1998 entering class—47 of these institutions being out of state."[20] Dean Walwer describes many Wesleyan students as non-traditional and seeking a legal education leading to public service. "The breadth and depth of such experiences provide an excellent background for classroom dialogue and substantially enrich our program."[21]

Walwer points to the newness of the school as an asset. "Thus, we have the fresh opportunity and flexibility to create a curriculum specifically designed to prepare our graduates with the knowledge, skills and professional insights required for the resolution of society's legal problems in the next century."[22]

Full-time students' first-semester courses include Analysis, Research & Writing; Civil Procedure; Contracts I; Introduction to Law; Property I; and Torts I. Second semester they enroll for Level II of these courses, with Criminal Law taking the place of Civil Law.

A visitor sitting in on a Torts class taught by Professor Earl Martin would see twenty to twenty-five casually dressed students, chattering as they entered the thirty-five-by-forty-foot classroom. Backpacks and commercial bottles of water or canned soft drinks share space on their tables with thick textbooks and notepads. Most students look to be twenty-five to thirty years old, but a few are definitely older. All are seriously attentive when Professor Martin announces the case to be discussed. He knows each student by name and calls on different ones to tell what the court ruling in the case being considered is, and the legal basis for the decision. The give and take between professor and students is friendly as he leads them to think of different possibilities, but all based on case law. "How would you argue this as a ..." he keeps pulling, pulling to elicit answers. "Then what? ..."

Third-semester courses for full-time students are Business Associations, Constitutional Law, and Estate Planning I (Estates and Trusts). The same courses are divided into four semesters for part-time students.

Degrees are conferred on those who successfully (passing grade of 70) complete an eighty-

Professor Earl F. Martin teaches Criminal Law, Torts, and Death Penalty. Professor of the Year 1997-1998.
—Photo courtesy TWU School of Law

Student presents his case in "Moot Court."
—Photo courtesy of TWU School of Law

eight-unit course of study. The day division students taking the fourteen-week fall and spring semester course load of thirteen to sixteen hours graduate in three years. Evening division students cover the units over a four-year period. An externship allows students to work with practicing attorneys.

In the on-site law clinic students represent indigent clients, again under the supervision of a faculty advisor. "The law clinic is an actual law office operated by law students and a faculty supervisor," according to the booklet, *Programs, Policies & Procedures*.[23]

Practicing attorneys see the law school as an excellent source of part-time clerks. "They get to see how a law firm operates and we have an opportunity to get to know them and how well they work. It's much better than a two hour interview," said one well respected lawyer.[24] It is not uncommon for firms to offer employment to former clerks after they graduate.

Texas Wesleyan University School of Law offers students multiple opportunities for socialization while augmenting their education. Organizations such as the Asian & Pacific Law Student Association, Black Law School Association, Hispanic Law Students Association, Jewish Law Students Association, and the Organization of Women Law Students, as the names imply, are geared to serve subgroups of students. The Christian Legal Society promotes Christian values among students. For those interested in politics there are the Law Democrats and Law Republicans Associations. Alternative Dispute Resolutions Bar, Environmental Law Society, Mock Trial Association, and Tax & Estate Planning Society give students of like interests a format for interaction. All are encouraged to join the Student Bar Association.

Lex Et Veritas, the student newspaper, provides news of students and faculty. The book store, two blocks north at 1313 Calhoun, stocks new and used textbooks, study aids, code books, office supplies, and law-related gifts. Law school students are eligible to use the wide range of recreational and sports facilities on the main campus. The university's health center, located in the Sid W. Richardson Center on the main campus, provides for routine health needs.

One of the most cherished traditions at Texas Wesleyan University is the Robing Ceremony. Shortly before graduation, black-robed seniors stand before the professors of their choice, to be draped with the colored hood of their school. It is an emotional culmination of years of friendship, mentoring, and study. Handshakes and hugs abound, and tears are not uncommon. The tradition now includes the law school. In December and May ceremonies, candidates for the juris doctor stand before the dean who bestows upon the proud students their academic hoods.

What does the future hold for graduates? Associate Dean Malinda Seymore hopes many will make legal services available to middle class citizens. "The poor can go to Legal Services, the wealthy have lawyers to handle their complex estates: those in the middle who just need legal advice on a simple contract, will, or other minor business matter, should have affordable access to lawyers."[25] Her charge to graduates is to make a difference, little by little, in the social fabric of their own particular world.

Noting that not all graduates will practice law, trustee Gary Cumbie sees their education as a way to make their lives better.

Making a legal point.
—Photo courtesy TWU School of Law

Law school students listen and take notes.
—Photo courtesy of TWU School of Law

"Really, that's the thing that appeals to me most about the law school—a lot of folks ... don't intend to be lawyers, but they make themselves better equipped to do whatever they do by learning the law."[26]

As the time approached for the American Bar Association's Council of the Section on Legal Education and Admission to render a decision, the feeling of cautious optimism grew. It was replaced by spirited pride when Wesleyan received word of the August 10, 1999, approval. In a news release President Schrum and Dean Walwer noted the school became one of only 181 fully-approved law schools nationwide, and was now the first such law school in Fort Worth. "An air of celebration and relief filled the [Law School] courtroom on August 11 as University officials, local business leaders, law students, and alumni toasted President Jake B. Schrum's formal announcement that the American Bar Association (ABA) had granted full approval of the Texas Wesleyan University School of Law."[27]

TEXAS WESLEYAN UNIVERSITY
SCHOOL OF LAW
1998-1999 Faculty

Name	Law School Attended
Stephen R. Alton	LL.M., Columbia University
William M. Blackburn	LL.B., University of Texas, Honors
John C. Cady	J.D., George Washington University National Law Center, Highest Honors
Wylie Davis	LL.M., Harvard University
Howard A. Denemark	J.D., University of Wisconsin, Honors
Anthony M. Dillof	LL.M., Columbia University
John C. Duncan, Jr.	J.D., Yale University
Frank W. Elliott	LL.B., University of Texas, Honors
Cynthia L. Fontaine	J.D., University of Cincinnati
James Paul George	LL.M., Columbia University
L. Richard Gershon	LL.M., University of Florida
W. Robert Gray	J.D., University of Chicago
James Hambleton	J.D., George Washington University National Law Center
Gilbert Holmes	J.D., New York University
Charlotte A. Hughart	J.D., University of Oklahoma
Denny O. Ingram, Jr.	J.D., University of Texas, Honors
Jeffery A. Maine	LL.M., University of Florida
Earl F. Martin	LL.M., Yale University, Honors
Lynne H. Rambo	J.D., University of Georgia, magna cum laude
Ruth L. Rickard	LL.M., University of London (Queen Mary College)
Malinda L. Seymore	J.D., Baylor University cum laude
Joseph Shade	J.D., University of Texas, Honors
Joe Spurlock, II	LL.M., University of Virginia
Richard F. Storrow	J.D., Columbia University
Frank K. Walwer	LL.B., Columbia University
Donald Zahn	LL.M., New York University

1998-1999 Adjunct Faculty

Sue Allen
Geffrey Anderson
The Hon. Charles Bleil
Brian Bowden
Allen Butler
Perry Cockerell
Dennis Conrad
Ann Diamond
Patrick Dohoney
Kathi Drew
Kay Elkins-Elliott
The Hon. Gordon G. Gray
The Hon. Cheril Hardy
Maxine Harrington
Susan Heygood
The Hon. R. Brent Keis
The Hon. Ed Kindeade
Kathleen Kohl
Annette Loyd
Charles M. Mallen

Robert Martin, Jr.
The Hon. Robert McCoy
Randyl Meigs
The Hon. Joe Morris
Susan Phillips
Vickie Rainwater
Florintino Ramirez
The Hon. Barbara Rosenberg
Lee Schwemer
Joe Shannon, Jr.
Jeffrey Storie
Donald Teller, Jr.
Mark Thielman
The Hon. Linda Thomas
Thomas R. Trompeter
Behrooz Vida
R. K. Weaver
Michael Williams
Mark Zimmerman

PART THREE
The Halls of Justice

The Courthouses

On a crisp December day in 1983, United States House Majority Leader Jim Wright, Congressman Tom Vandergriff, Lt. Governor Bill Hobby, Speaker of the Texas House Gib Lewis, and Mayor Bob Bolen gathered to celebrate the facelift of a "Grand Old Lady." County Judge Mike Moncrief addressed the assembled group of dignitaries and citizens.

It was 90 years ago that this courthouse—the Tarrant County courthouse—rose from the North Texas prairie to stand as an enduring symbol of the spirit and hard work of the frontier men and women who built this community from the wilderness.

Today we rededicate this courthouse, not only as a symbol of Tarrant County's rebirth and continued progress, but also as a symbol of a past we respect and a legacy upon which we are proud to build.

When we open the doors of this building and walk inside, we will be stepping back 90 years in time. Try to imagine, if you can, what Tarrant County was like back in the 1890s and imagine also what this building—this courthouse—meant to the people who lived here around the turn of the century.

There were more than 40,000 people here then, and half in Fort Worth and the rest on the farms and in the communities that made up the remainder of Tarrant County. They were busy creating and building a new community, out of what, just a few short decades before, had been uncharted wilderness.

The first railroad had steamed into town on tracks laid by the people of Fort Worth with their own hands. Electricity and the telephone were both new inventions just starting to spread. The Tarrant County seat, Fort Worth, was just beginning to shed its raw frontier appearance and begin the long road toward becoming a truly great American city. The nineteenth century of cattle drives and stagecoaches was coming to an end and a new century, soon to be filled with horseless carriages and flying machines was about to begin.

Fort Worth was then an overgrown town in a far off corner of the country. It took a great deal of foresight and courage on the part of those who decided that this frontier city deserved such a magnificent building. For them, the construction of this courthouse symbolized the taming of the frontier and the bringing of justice to a land more famous for its saloons and gunfights than as a center of civilized behavior.

By building this courthouse, the people of Tarrant County showed the rest of Texas, as well as the country, that Tarrant County was an important place. While it may have been small, it was growing and the people here had big dreams and big plans. When it came to building our community, they went first class.

Of course, those who are familiar with Tarrant County history know that the county commissioners who authorized building this courthouse were, perhaps, a bit ahead of their time. At the very next election after the courthouse was finished they were all voted out of office by a citizenry who felt that Tarrant County would never live up to or need such a grand courthouse.

Somehow I know that if the men and women who lived in Tarrant County a century ago could come back and see this county today; could see the restored old buildings and gleaming new skyscrapers of downtown Fort Worth; could see what's going on in the very same stockyards that they once knew; could go further out and see Arlington Stadium and Six Flags; could see our aerospace factories and our international airport, the largest in the nation; could see our fine homes and schools and churches; could see our lakes and parks and museums; could really see how their plans for the growth of this county have blossomed and prospered, they would approve of this courthouse and what we have done to preserve it. They would agree that Tarrant County deserves this building as it originally stood.

If they could see what this county has become in the past 90 years, I know that they would be proud that this building still stands, and now restored, still graces our community.

All of us in Tarrant County can be proud of what we have achieved through this historic restoration. By continuing to work together, this county will serve as a shining example of what a community can achieve and preserve, not only for this generation, but for the many future generations to come.[1] (Used by permission.)

Tarrant County was separated from Navarro County in 1850. It was named for Edward H. Tarrant, who served under Andrew Jackson at New Orleans in the War of 1812. Tarrant joined the Texas Army twenty-three years later. "He was a Ranger, a congressman of the Republic, and in 1841 his victory at Village Creek caused the Indians to move westward and open Tarrant County to settlement."[2]

The history of the courthouse goes back further than the 100 W. Weatherford Street building. In 1856 not all the arguing, posturing, and wrangling had to do with trials. For years the debate was over the location of the courthouse. City fathers realized they must establish Fort Worth as the county seat to insure growth or even survival, but Birdville was the site of the courthouse at what is now approximately the 6100 block of Broadway in Haltom City.

A delegation of Fort Worth citizens convinced the state legislature to call a special election to determine which village should be designated the county seat.

On the day of the November election, Fort Worth was bustling with men ready to do their civic duty. Fortified by the barrels of whiskey two merchants had thoughtfully provided, they drank, voted, drank some more, and waited for the final tally. In Birdville the scene was duplicated, except for the availability of whiskey. "In the darkness of election eve, a band of Fort Worth men had stolen into (Birdville) and siphoned the whiskey into their own barrel, leaving Birdville without a lure for voters."[3]

Election officials kept a running tally of votes, and when it appeared Fort Worth was running behind, riders were sent out to bring friendly voters to the polls. One such friendly voter was Sam Woody. The only problem was Sam recently had moved from Tarrant County to Wise County. Many years later he told the story. "Around me were fourteen other settlers, and on the day of the election I got them together and started down to Fort Worth to help my former fellow citizens get what they wanted."[4] His biggest problem was keeping his voting bloc away from the free whiskey. He warned, "Boys, we've got to stay sober 'til this election is over. I must vote every one of you, so we must hold in 'til we get home. It is a penitentiary offense, and if they find us defrauding the ballot we will have to leave home for several years."[5] That unwelcome prospect, and Woody's strict control, kept them in line. At the polls, they pretended to be in a big hurry, needing only to cast their ballot and get on about their business. None was challenged concerning his residency.

Fort Worth won by seven votes. When the votes were canvassed officials discovered more votes had been cast than were citizens of the county. Birdville protested. Fort Worth celebrated.

Immediately following the election, the biggest party Fort Worth had ever witnessed took place on the bluff overlooking the Trinity. Huge bonfires lit up the night skies and more whiskey was consumed. "Escorted by torchbearing merrymakers, a wagon was driven to Birdville and there loaded with record books, antiquated desks, cane bottom chairs, and yellowed law books, all of which were hauled away in a serpentine torchlight parade while glum Birdville residents watched."[6]

It took four years for Birdville to win a new election. By that time their rival for the county seat had seen tremendous growth. The Fort Worth-Jacksboro Stage Line had begun connecting with the Butterfield Overland Stage Line, and many of those making the stop liked what they saw and stayed. The new, and legal, count stood at 548 for Fort Worth, 301 for an undesignated "center of the county," and only four votes for Birdville.

It was not until 1947 that the deed of the site of the old Birdville courthouse was legally cleared. William Norris bought the property in 1871. But the deed was either never filed or was destroyed when the courthouse burned in 1876. Later it was purchased by Edward Hovenkamp. His February 22, 1877, deed was in question until the Commissioners' Court approved a quit-claim deed seventy years after the purchase.

The legal sanction for Tarrant County reads: "The Texas

Legislature passed an Act September 4, 1850 which read: 'Sec. 2: Be it further enacted. That the several courts for said county shall be at the store house of E. M. Daggete [sic], in the vicinity of Fort Worth, until the election provided for in the first section of this bill have been holden, and the county seat permanently located.'"[7] Actually it was the store run by Henry Daggett, for E. M. Daggett had not opened a store at that time. The first recorded session was held under a giant oak tree in front of Henry's store. Judge Oran Roberts, who became governor in 1879, presided. The session lasted two days and dealt with six indictments which had been handed down by the grand jury. Three cases involved assault, not uncommon on the frontier. Of a more serious nature were the cases involving fire. One, arson of a house, was probably the result of a feud. The other two, firing of the prairie, were considered potentially catastrophic owing to the lack of any means to control a runaway fire. John H. Reagan, later postmaster of the Confederate States of America, and General Tarrant participated in the trials.

Fort Worth's first two-story building went up in 1856. It housed a general store at ground level and space was provided on the second floor for a courtroom. Records show 280 men were eligible for jury duty in the new quarters.

The following year E. M. Daggett agreed to build a free standing courthouse. Like other frontier buildings—a small dog-trot cabin—it had rooms on either side of the breezeway for storing legal records and holding court. Its breezeway became infamous as the haven for drunks and stray hogs.

One of the more memorable trials in this courthouse was that of Dr. Mansell Mathews, a traveling evangelist. During the Civil War, vigilante committees ruled the land. Mathews was arrested by Southern sympathizers, then tried and convicted of treason against the Confederacy. E. M. Daggett intervened on the popular preacher's behalf, and the death sentence was commuted to three days in jail without the accused knowing his fate. "Daggett thought the edict was cruel, and determined to tell Mathews."[8] He was allowed to visit the condemned man, but only with a jailer present. During the conversation, Daggett asked Mathews his favorite scripture. Mathews in turn asked Daggett's favorite. Relying on the ignorance of the jailer,

Daggett responded, "Fret not thy gizzard and frizzle not thy whirligig, thou soul art saved."[9] The preacher wisely hid any emotion upon hearing the news of his good fortune. The jailer's reaction to the "scripture" was not reported.

In 1856 one of the most important factors that swayed voters was the promise of thirty-eight Fort Worth men to pay for the construction of a new courthouse. After the 1860 election, with their town unquestionably the county seat, David Mauck, one of the backers, led with a donation of $250.00. E. L. Terrill, N. Terry, and T. O. Moody each gave $200.00. Those giving $150.00 each were L. Terry, and A. Goehenunt. One hundred dollar donors were C. M. Peak, L. Steel, and A. D. Johnson. Fourteen citizens gave $50.00 and fifteen men donated $25.00 each. With the money in hand, they began work on the first "real" courthouse.

A copy of an official courthouse document shows the specifications.

> The house to be fifty by sixty feet built upon the present foundation as now laid for the outside walls of said building.
> The foundation of the inside walls to be dug out down to the rock and laid 18 inches in thickness up to a level with the present stone foundation for the outside walls. From this foundation the first story is to be thirteen feet high from floor to floor. The outside walls to be 18 inches in thickness; the inside walls to be 13½ inches in thickness. One door and two windows in each outside wall—dimensions hereinafter specified and one door to each of the court rooms in the inside walls. Four rooms—one in each corner of the house. Cross alleys through running from east to west 15 feet wide. The one from north to south 16 feet wide. The walls to be laid with the faced finish outside—inside common finish of true walls. The brick to be grossed or tied every fifth course.[10]

The document continues to spell out exact dimensions and requirements.

The last paragraph states the contract for building had been given to David Mauck. ". . . and said Mauck having given bond and surety for the performance of the same is hereby agreed to by all the parties in this contract. . . ."[11] Slave labor was used to erect the stone, tin-roofed structure until work was halted when war broke out between the states.

K. M. Van Zandt, in 1865, wrote, "The town had been laid out according to the general style, with a square in the center and stores surrounding it. A courthouse had been started in 1860. The rock walls had been built up as high as the first story, and there the work had stopped."[12] He went on to describe the desolation he saw in the once bustling town.

The economy slowly rebounded and the courthouse was finished in 1866. Tragedy struck in the dreaded form of fire ten years later. The *Democrat* on March 29, 1876, reported:

"BLAZES
Court House Burned!
TOTAL DESTRUCTION OF
THE COUNTY RECORDS
LOSS INCALCULABLE!"

The origin of the blaze was unknown, but believed to have started in the office of the clerk of the District Court. Fire was spotted between four and five in the morning and confined mainly to the records area. Editor B. B. Paddock noted, "Had the records of the courts been saved, the loss would have been slight. . . ."[13]

Then an amazing thing happened. Attorneys got together and for six to eight weeks re-constructed deeds and records from their personal files and recollections. Local historian Quentin McGown said, "Researchers today will find records sworn to by those who preserved materials which would have been lost forever."[14]

After the fire, the county rented the Darter Building on Houston Street for one month to use as a courthouse. In a memo to Judge Steve King, Dee Baker of the Tarrant County Historical Society wrote, "A frame building 25x60 feet was built on the edge of the square to serve as the county Court House while the stone Court House was being constructed."[15]

The Fort Worth *Standard* reported on November 3, 1876, "The old Courthouse has been torn down and a great pile of 'gray sad rocks' is all that remains of the grim old ruins from this whilom temple of justice."[16]

Citizens were polled and most agreed a new, bigger and better courthouse should be built on the same site. Commissioners studied several buildings, including the state capitol. They chose to model the new courthouse after the building in Austin.

The architectural firm of Gunn and Curtiss provided the design and on April 22, 1883, they were paid $2,500. Probst Construction Company was awarded the building contract. Commissioners allocated $500,000 for the edifice. The exact bid was for $408,840, but they decided to leave out elevators at a saving of $4,636. Another $2,064 was cut when they substituted cement for mosaic tile on the basement floor.

Designed in a French-influenced Renaissance Revival style, the courthouse's pink granite walls are five feet thick at their base. Area within the walls measures 114,211 square feet. The highest point, at the top of the clock tower, is just over 193 feet, seven inches, from the ground. Only the structural steel and glass windows came from outside the state. Judge King, in his booklet, *A Walking Tour of the Courthouse*, noted, "The construction of the Courthouse was pioneering in the use of concrete and steel. The steel columns and beams throughout the building were encased in clay tile for protection from fire." [17]

The building was designed much like other Texas courthouses, the cross-shaped structure measured fifty by sixty feet, with a domed central axis and a lantern atop the dome. "The Courthouse Plaza is laid out on two city blocks . . . the focal point both from downtown to the South as well as from below the Trinity River Bluff to the North." [18] The square around the building was formed by the dusty streets of Belknap, Houston, Rusk, and Weatherford. Rusk later became Commerce Street.

"When the cornerstone was laid . . . in a copper box [were placed] a bottle of Tarrant County wine, local newspapers, photographs of downtown buildings, a list of courthouse employees, rosters of local fraternities, church membership lists, membership of the local chapter of the Grand Army of the Republic, $100.00 in Confederate money, 1847 and 1894 copper pennies, and a lock of hair from a child of County Judge Robert G. Johnson." [19]

The Commissioners' Court was called into special session Saturday, June 29, 1895, to formally receive the new building. "A section of the official record of that session is headed 'Court

Tarrant County Courthouse, 1894
—Photo courtesy W. D. Smith

House.' This record says the Probst Construction Company was anxious to deliver to Tarrant County the Court House it constructed and thereby relieve itself of the responsibility of caring for and keeping the Court House. . . ."[20] Like new construction today, there were small problems. The dome leaked, the doors to the Criminal Court rooms needed adjusting, and some painting was yet to be done. Clear glass had been installed where stained glass was called for and had to be changed out, but on the condition that these matters be corrected, the courthouse was accepted.

On July 1, 1895, the Court of Appeals was given permission to move into the new quarters. "The courthouse today is home to the Second Court of Appeals," according to Judge King, "one District Court, two Probate Courts, three County Courts at Law and one Justice of the Peace Court."[21] Also housed there are the county clerk's office, elections administration offices, a constable's office, and the law library.

The 1895 courthouse was one of the finest structures of its time, but the fickle public deplored the cost. They also complained it was so big it would never be fully occupied. In anger, they voted out of office every commissioner who had complied with their earlier wishes to build a "grand" courthouse.

By 1941 not the building, but the horseless, waterless water trough on the southeast corner of the courthouse grounds was the subject of controversy. The old water trough, once the pride of all lovers of horseflesh and the oasis for humble nags and proud trotters, had fallen into near ruin. It had been a gift given in 1892 by the Woman's Humane Association, forerunner of the Fort Worth Humane Society. Women representing the Tarrant County Historical Society and various other civic organizations demanded to know what had happened to the bronze horse which once rested atop the dried-up fountain. Commissioners explained the statue had been removed when they feared it might jar loose from its crumbling base and fall on someone. "Where is it now?" they asked. The women were told it was put in storage at the Lucas Funeral Home. Bob Lucas entered the fray by asking to be reimbursed for the $10.00 it cost him to remove it.

The commissioners assured the indignant group they wanted to restore the landmark, but must follow procedures. Judge Dave Miller vowed no one was more interested in seeing the marker preserved. "Why as a boy I admired that fountain and wanted to ride that bronze horse—and I did." One of the women, observing the portly judge, wondered what he weighed as a boy and suggested "maybe that's what shook the horse loose from the pedestal."[22]

The order to destroy the trough was rescinded, but repairs

The controversial waterless horse trough on the courthouse grounds, circa 1940.

—Photo courtesy UTA
Special Collection Library

were never made. Three years later the subject of the horseless landmark was cautiously broached. County Judge Clarence Kraft asked for a motion to remove the mass of deteriorated red sandstones. "'It's an eyesore,' he declared. Commissioner Frank Winters chimed in calling it a bottle catcher. 'It's a mosquito trap' joined in Commissioner Joe Thannisch."[23] Civic leader Miss Margaret McLean argued for the restoration, but County Engineer Steve Champeaux ruled it a safety hazard. A compromise was worked out whereby the pillars on which the horse had rested were removed. The landmark lasted a few more years until finally it was bulldozed to make way for the 1950 era courthouse expansion.

As part of the sesquicentennial celebration, a new 25-foot pink granite and limestone fountain, complete with a prancing cast aluminum horse, was unveiled June 4, 1999. Judge Pat Ferchill presided over the ceremony as Mrs. W. K. Gordon, Jr. officially reopened the horse fountain on the east lawn of the Tarrant County Courthouse. The horse is named "Penny's Worth" in recognition of the thousands of pennies collected by school children to help pay for the restoration.

A 1944 addition to the courthouse was the Tarrant County Law Library. Sponsored by the county bar association, its first librarian was George W. Steere. Steere, a graduate of the old Fort Worth University Law School, directed the shelving and furniture placement. Later, the 45,000-volume library was named the Dell DeHay Library of Tarrant County. DeHay had been its longtime librarian. Open to the public as well as lawyers, it is housed on the fourth floor.

Even with the addition of the library and other courts, it took fifty years for the venerable 1894 building at the north end of downtown to be filled to overflowing. Newspaper accounts in the 1940s told of crowded conditions and crumbling fixtures. Also noted was the wrangling over building plans and finances. In late 1941 workmen started on the $50,000 remodeling project. Six months later County Auditor J. M. (Star) Williams reported that almost daily expansions of the original plans had bumped the cost up to $115,000. One of the reasons for the increased cost was the problem with the roof. Commissioners had to choose between the lesser of two evils. They could remove

15,000 pounds of rickety ornamental iron, and possibly significantly damage the roof, or leave the iron and risk it falling onto the third floor of the courthouse. They opted to remove the iron.

Not all of the remodeling was structural. The courthouse clock was repaired. The Seth Thomas timepiece had quite a history. It was new when Fort Worth boys joined Teddy Roosevelt to fight in the Spanish-American War. The big three-ton bell in the tower tolled at 11:00 A.M. on November 11, 1918, and its hands were pointing to 12:30 P.M. on December 7, 1941, when America was plunged into World War II. But it quit November 7, 1944.

A crew from the I. T. Verdin Clock Company of Cincinnati was called in to make the repairs. It took a week for the workmen to repaint the iron numerals on the twelve-foot dial, and install new glass on the face. The internal works, once powered by heavy weights which were pulled laboriously to the top of the thirty-foot shaft, were replaced by a small electric motor.

They knew what time it was, but for the rest of the decade, workers in the courthouse complained of cramped conditions. In 1947 probate clerk Tommy Thompson couldn't find counter space to look into one of his huge record books—he had to lay it on the floor in order to thumb through the pages. Others told similar horror stories, while commissioners pondered, asked for suggestions, and delayed.

Groups speaking for adding new floors to the existing building sparred with groups opting to erect new or additional buildings. A committee of North Side businessmen suggested tearing down the courthouse and opening Main Street to their area of town. Preservationists such as Miss McLean pleaded with commissioners to save and restore the historic building. Lawyers put in their two cents worth. Frank Taylor, president of the Tarrant County Bar Association, pledged the cooperation of his colleagues, but warned they were very much against any large-scale remodeling of the present courthouse.

Cosmetic changes were made in the early fifties and not to everyone's liking. In September 1952 a longtime tradition was shattered. Domino players were ousted from the courthouse. For as long as anyone could remember the petit jury room in the basement was the scene of serious shuffling of the bones. "The oldsters passed the word through County Judge Brown to

Commissioners Court that they were double blank as far as playing sites were concerned." When a commissioner suggested a domino parlor, "'Yes, but that costs 10 cents a game,' said Judge Brown."[24]

That same week the County Health Department posted bright yellow signs outlawing spitting on the floor or steps. Next to go were the spittoons, replaced with clean cylinders filled with sand. Perhaps the tobacco chewers brought it on themselves, since the complaint inferred chewers couldn't spit as accurately as in the old days. Commissioner C. H. (Punch) Wright, known to "chaw a little," said, "It shore ain't like it used to be when I was a youngster. When a boy got 17 and old enough to chew, he was taken out in the country and there he fired away at tin cans. He wasn't allowed to spit in public until he could hit a tin can at 20 paces."[25]

The most visible cosmetic change was the neon American flag. The American Legion's Bothwell Kane Post offered to raise the money and erect the flag at no cost to the taxpayers. The 1,250-pound flag, six by ten feet, had a rippled effect and rotated on a mast affixed to the courthouse dome. Forty-eight stars and thirteen stripes were formed by 775 bulbs of appropriate colors. The lights were turned on at dusk each day until 1959, when commissioners voted unanimously to have what some considered an embarrassment removed. The stars of Alaska and Hawaii, admitted to the Union that year, never lighted the Fort Worth sky. A more conventional flag, with fifty stars, now flies from a pole near the front steps. A quarter of a century later, a *Star-Telegram* reporter wrote, "In a windblown morning ceremony, Tarrant County officials helped dedicate two new flagpoles in front of the courthouse to attorney Forrest Markward." Tom Vandergriff helped unveil the plaque that lauds Markward as "Attorney at Law, gentleman of the old school, lest we forget."[26]

In 1954 a state constitutional amendment was proposed to allow women to serve on juries. It was supported by the League of Women Voters and the Business and Professional Women's Club of Fort Worth. Mrs. George W. Stevens spoke for the League and attorney Eva Barnes, Jefferson Law School graduate and chair of the B&PW legislative committee, voiced her group's recommendation for approval.

The women had two judges on their side. Criminal District Court Judge Willis McGregor declared, "there is no good reason for excluding women from jury service."[27] District Judge Langdon agreed. "Women of Texas are entitled to full citizenship," he said.[28] The amendment passed.

The change in the law was a spur to major changes at the courthouse; there were no women's restrooms in the jury rooms. Proponents of a new building to house modern courts saw this as ammunition for their side in the ongoing battle of how to resolve the overcrowding. Instead minor changes were made, and women jurors had their restrooms.

Forty-five years later it was the dress code for female attorneys and witnesses that caused a short-term but heated discussion at the court of U. S. Bankruptcy Judge Massie Tillman. On March 15, 1999, he ruled that women must wear skirts and blouses or dresses in his courtroom. There was an outcry from women accustomed to wearing tailored pants suits. An Op-Ed piece in the *Fort Worth Star-Telegram* suggested that male attorneys and witnesses be required to wear spats and cutaway coats. Not surprisingly, that piece was written by a female columnist. A week later the judge wisely made another ruling. "In light of what has transpired in the wake of my amendment to my Local/Local Rules regarding women's dress code, I have concluded that it was probably the wrong thing to do and it is hereby rescinded."[29]

Concerning the Tarrant County courthouse, after years of discussion, commissioners agreed to build a new Civil Courts Building, just west of the century-old edifice. At a cost of $2.5 million, it was finished in 1958. The Criminal Courts Building and jail is located at 401 W. Weatherford. A new jail was built in 1963 and cost approximately $1,000,000 more than the Civil Courts Building.

In early 1980 significant restoration of the courthouse began. Ward Bogard and Associates, Burson, Hendricks & Walls, Architects, Inc., and Walker Construction Company were selected based on their reputable work in the restoration of older and historical structures. A first order of business was to rid the copper dome of its numerous coats of aluminum paint. The exterior was cleaned by water-blasting a combination restoration cleaner and hot water under high pressure. Windows were cleaned and duplicated in their original style. Modern heating and central air-conditioning were installed. Throughout the building electrical and plumbing fixtures were upgraded.

Cast bronze doorknobs, with the unusual Tarrant County signature in bright brass, graced the doors. Tall hallways of marble wainscoting and plaster were repaired and cleaned. Mack Williams, in a story headlined "Here's to a Grand Old Lady," described the interior. "The courthouse has 27.36 miles of wood trim and 3.4 miles of plaster moldings. Every inch was polished or painted."[30]

Today's visitors see replicated terazzo floors leading to the central rotunda. The rotunda, measuring 110 feet from the main floor to the interior dome, features an illuminated stained glass county seal. The seal, composed of an olive branch and oak leaves, is six feet in diameter. Symmetrical staircases, with ornate railings, surround the rotunda on its east and west sides. Located in the rotunda on the first floor is a sculpture, *Free Legal Advice*. It was donated by Lex Graham, the sculptor, in 1983.

In the remodeling, courtrooms were refinished with solid oak backdrops. Benches and other mill work were restored and refinished. Egg and dart moulding was used in the rooms. The courthouse truly was a "Grand Old Lady" heading into the next millennium.

It was announced March 24, 1999, that the architectural firm of Gideon-Toal was selected to design a new law center and multi-story parking garage to be built east of the historic courthouse. It will house civil and family courts. Stressing the importance of compatibility with existing structures, spokesman David M. Schwartz assured commissioners, "It must be a 'good neighbor' to the old courthouse, and be easily accessible to the public, humane, yet not detract from the majesty of the law."[31]

Whatever the additions, as Judge Moncrief so confidently proclaimed, "By working together, this county will serve as a shining example of what a community can achieve and preserve, not only for this generation, but for the many future generations to come."[32]

Carnage at the Courthouse

It was already getting to be a scorcher that first day of July 1992 when George Douglas Lott calmly entered the Tarrant County Courthouse. Neatly dressed in a blue coat, tan pants, white shirt and red tie, Lott carried a briefcase into the Second Court of Appeals courtroom on the fourth floor and sat down. He looked like any other lawyer—in fact he was a lawyer. At approximately 10:00 A.M. he drew a Glock 9mm semiautomatic pistol, advanced toward the three-judge panel, and starting firing. Before he mingled with the crush of terrified county employees being evacuated from the courthouse, he had killed two men and wounded three others.

Lott, forty-five years old, was no longer a practicing attorney. He identified himself as a computer programmer, but was believed to be living off his rather substantial inheritance. He bore no grudge against the men he shot: they were merely symbols of a court system he had grown to hate.

Fort Worth attorney Daniel Hollifield was arguing a routine issue in a misdemeanor case before Judges David Farris, John Hill, and Clyde Ashworth in the Second Court of Appeals. Steve Conder, newly hired by the district attorney, had presented the case for the prosecution. Chris Marshall, Condor's supervisor, was in the courtroom to observe the young man. There were other lawyers and some spectators in the room when Lott opened fire.

A newspaper reporter detailed Hollifield's firsthand description of the event. "I had been up on my feet talking for about five minutes when I heard a loud noise, then another one, and turned around to see a man pointing a gun at the front of the courtroom and firing."[1]

Hollifield, unharmed, rushed through what he hoped was a door leading out of the courtroom. Instead, it led into an adjacent room where he remained until the shooting stopped. He tried to call 911, but not being familiar with the telephone system, he didn't know he had to dial 89 to get an outside line. When he returned to the scene of the shooting, he saw Judge Clyde Ashworth lying wounded, an unnamed woman trying to comfort him.

State District Judge Ashworth had retired six years earlier. He had been a part of the legal community for thirty-five years, first as an Arlington attorney, then judge of the Sixty-seventh District Court of Tarrant County, and later was an associate justice in the State Court of Appeals. Occasionally he filled in for ill or vacationing judges, as he was doing the day of the shooting.

The sixty-nine-year-old jurist was lying on a step behind the bench, shot twice in the buttocks. The injuries left him temporarily paralyzed and confined to a wheelchair. He later regained mobility, but wore a brace on his lower right leg. Longtime friend, State Representative Doyle Willis, thought it bizarre that Ashworth, a former Marine who saw duty in World War II and the Korean War, would be wounded in a court of law.

Hal Lattimore, another Second Court of Appeals judge, was in his office when he heard the shots. He went into the courtroom and noticed five empty 9mm shell casings on the floor. He noted that Judge John Hill, forty-eight years old, had rolled under the judges' bench.

Hill suffered a bruised shoulder blade, broken ribs, and a punctured lung. He fully recovered from his wounds.

Assistant District Attorney Steve Conder, youngest of the wounded men, was grazed in the chest. Not so fortunate were C. Chris Marshall and John J. Edwards.

Marshall, forty-one, was the chief appellate prosecutor in the district attorney's office. He was sitting on the right side of the courtroom in one of the middle rows, following the arguments of Conder. Fatally shot in the face and back, he was found on the floor of the west side of the spectator section.

Assistant District Attorney Steve Chaney was one of many who grieved at the death of Marshall. Chaney, best man at Chris's wedding to attorney Betty Stanton Marshall, described his friend as a brilliant scholar who was well respected for his ability to make sense of the law. "Chris Marshall was the smartest lawyer I've ever known as far as his insights into the law and his knowledge of it," Chaney said.[2]

Other attorneys, such as Don Hase, praised the slain man as friendly and "a person of principle, highly moral, highly religious, but very modest and unassuming and not aggressive in any way."[3] Prior to his employment in the district attorney's office, Marshall practiced as a trial lawyer in partnership with his father, Clyde Marshall.

Dallas resident Edwards, thirty-three years old, was hit by six bullets as he tried to leave the courthouse. His body lay on the stairs outside the courtroom.

Another Dallas attorney, Keith Jenson, heard a half dozen or so shots as he was leaving a nearby restroom. "They clearly came from the stairwell leading to the fourth floor. I believe those were the shots that killed the attorney [Edwards] I was scheduled to argue against in the next hearing."[4]

State Representative Toby Goodman had just left the courtroom and was getting on an elevator when he heard gunfire. "I saw somebody in a blue blazer running down the stairs and out the other end of the building."[5]

Lawyer Nelda Harris was in a second-floor probate court. She reported hearing "a pop like a car backfire, then the rapid rattle of five or seven bullets."[6] Years later she recalled it as the most horrifying experience of her life. "We (she and four or five other people) rushed into the office of the probate court in which Pat Furchill presides and barricaded the door. We didn't know what was happening, who was shooting or where the shooter was. We tried to call 911 but the lines were busy."[7] The group huddled in the office for what seemed like hours, but it was only thirty minutes before sheriff's deputies told them it was safe to come out.

As Harris and others were trying to call 911, Lott concealed his weapon and walked by a court bailiff who was ushering everyone out of the building. Little is known of the killer's whereabouts or actions from that time until six hours later.

At 4:15 that afternoon Lott walked into the Dallas television station WFAA/Channel 8 and asked to speak to anchor Tracy Rowlett. Still armed, he spoke on tape, saying, "I was shooting at the bench and the judges."[8] He indicated his anger was toward the judicial system, not the people he killed. Then he continued, "There were several people in the courtroom. . . . I basically went in the courtroom and sat a while and then got up and shot apparently five people. One of them got up and started running out of the room. He was in front of me on the way I was going. I was shooting at the court, essentially, but other people got in the way or did things . . . ," he rambled on to the television anchor.[9]

Following his lengthy and often times disjointed confession, he was disarmed and arrested.

Lott's bitterness stemmed from a 1990 divorce in which Judge Maryellen Hicks granted custody of the Lott boy to his mother. At that time a court-appointed psychologist testified Lott suffered from paranoid delusions. This conclusion was based partly on the man's declaration he had hired a private detective to follow his wife's lawyer. Although Lott's license to practice law had expired without being renewed, he represented himself in the divorce proceedings and the appeal of Judge Hicks's ruling.

Lott had run afoul of the courts in a child custody case heard in an Illinois courtroom. Mrs. Lott alleged her husband abused their five-year-old son. She produced pictures of the boy's wounds after being sodomized with a gun and a knife. The color prints showed outlines of bruises where ropes cut into his thighs. The mother related her son's terror of his father as he described cult-like rituals and warnings that his mother would be killed if he told of "their little secrets." He recounted how his father would put the gun to his head and threaten to kill him.

Mrs. Lott knew the threats were real. "During her brief marriage and subsequent divorce proce ''ngs . . . Lott had shown a frightening appetite for pain, she saia. `ut when it suited his purposes, he presented such a well-adjusted public demeanor that no one would believe her cries for help. With the aid of the pictures, she convinced Peoria Judge Richard Grawey to place a restraining order allowing Lott to see his son only in the presence of a caseworker.

Lott also represented himself in Illinois, contending he was the victim of judicial corruption. The lawyer-turned-computer programmer told Judge Grawey he had not been able to present all his evidence. "Her lawyer was the son of a senior district divorce-court judge, and while he did not try the case, he did not have to try the case," Lott testified.[11] Several times Grawey reminded Lott his statements were not relevant to the case, and that the court found them offensive.

The Texan lost, and in the April prior to the July massacre, he was charged with aggravated sexual assault and scheduled for a July 20 trial in Peoria. He steadfastly maintained his innocence.

Early on the morning of the shooting, Lott telephoned Peoria County Clerk Michell Pratt, demanding that she drop the charges against him. Pratt replied that as a clerk she was not authorized to do so. "He just screamed and screamed and screamed at me about wanting the charges dropped."[12] About an hour later, his revenge set in motion badly needed changes in courthouse security.

Lott's trial was moved to Amarillo because of intense Fort Worth coverage of the shootings. Although his behavior, such as refusing to shed his prison garb and making obscene remarks, was considered strange, he was certified as competent to stand trial.

Prosecutor Alan Levy presented evidence of the defendant's history of explosive rages and threats of violence against anyone he felt wronged him. Often he railed against the legal system, alleging that without money to buy judges there was no way to win a case, one witness testified.

Levy closed his arguments by reminding jurors Lott entered the courtroom with five clips of ammunition and intended to use as many as possible in his murderous wrath. "He came to kill and be killed. Ladies and gentlemen, George Douglas Lott is guilty of capital murder."[13]

Lott presented a brief and muddled defense. Despite seven eyewitnesses identifying him as the shooter, he maintained he had been sitting outside the Court of Appeals moments before the shooting occurred, but left when he heard the shots. He explained his appearance at Channel 8 as a desire to get publicity about the unfairness of the court system. He suggested those who identified him confused his television image with that of the courtroom killer.

Prosecutor Mike Parrish countered by asking, "How come his Glock fired the twenty-one shell casings found at the scene?"

George Lott was convicted by a Potter County jury February 12, 1993. In the punishment phase of the trial three jail officials told of his frequent violent outbursts in which he cursed them and called them obscene names. But it was the chilling testimony of his ex-wife that prompted jurors to sentence Lott to death. Speaking publicly for the first time, she related physical and emotional abuse of both her and her son at the hands of the defendant. "The more she hurt, the more he liked it."[14] She warned that should he ever be released from prison, he would kill again. Prosecutor Levy supported the woman's assessment. "Mr. Lott radiates hate like an oven radiates heat."[15]

The jury deliberated slightly more than an hour before declaring Lott must die for his deadly rampage. As he had the previous day when the jury found him guilty, the condemned man showed no emotion upon hearing his fate.

Samuel Burton of Amarillo, speaking for the jurors, said the state's wealth of evidence played a primary role in their deliberations. They did not question Lott's guilt, but it was difficult for some to arrive at the death penalty. It was the "nature of the crime" and the "ruthlessness with which he committed it" that swayed the reluctant members of the panel, Burton explained.

Lott did not appeal his conviction. A lead story in the September 20, 1994, *Fort Worth Star-Telegram* noted "George Douglas Lott, an Arlington attorney who gunned down five people, killing two, in the Tarrant County Courthouse in 1992, had no final statement before he was executed by lethal injection early today."[16] Prison officials, state attorneys, and reporters witnessed the execution. They were joined by two ministers who had befriended Lott during his short stay on Death Row.

After extensive therapy, the boy whose custody case triggered so much bloodshed is doing well in a new environment with his mother.

More than one hundred years ago, when the courthouse was built in the late 1870s, men commonly wore guns strapped on their hips. But to the designers of the building, security was not an issue. It was built to be as accessible to citizens as possible. After the traumatic July 1992 shooting, courthouse employees again pointed out the need for greater protection.

For years judges and attorneys complained that it was too easy for angry or disturbed people to enter the courthouse and violently settle what they saw as an injustice. At the time of the Lott massacre, seventy-three deputies were assigned full-time bailiff duty, but they were ill-equipped to handle hostage-takers or spectators who suddenly opened fire in a courtroom.

There was confusion about the presence of a bailiff when Marshall and Edwards were killed. Daniel Hollifield told reporter Jeff Guinn, "There was no bailiff there. . . . I'm accustomed to seeing one. I know bailiffs are there more as an usher than for protection, but that's still someone in a uniform. This conflicted with the account by acting Sheriff Jim Minter, who said an armed bailiff was in the courtroom during the shootings."[17]

Lott was not the first in recent years to settle a personal grudge at the courthouse. In June 1986 an angry Domingo "Chico" Velasquez shot Harry L. Walker II point-blank in the back. The feud was longstanding. For months Velasquez had stalked his estranged wife and the victim. The day of the shooting he encountered them in County Criminal Court No. 2, where Walker was on trial for pointing a gun at Velasquez's son. After killing Walker, he took Juanita Velasquez hostage. He was wrestled to the floor and disarmed, but not before firing several shots at attorneys and law officials. He was sentenced to life in prison for the killing.

Three years later more blood pooled in the halls of justice. On August 1, 1989, Manuel "Manny" Cabano killed his girlfriend Juanita Hermosillo, then took his own life. As in the Lott case, sexual abuse of a child was the fuse attached to a powder keg of violence. Hermosillo charged Cabano, a former sheriff's deputy turned private investigator, with abusing her daughter.

On the day of the shooting Cabano sealed himself and Hermosillo in the office of Justice of the Peace Robert Ashmore, where the woman worked. Negotiations failed and Cabano shot Hermosillo in the chest, then placed the .44 Magnum to his chin and fired.

After both incidents, suggestions were made, both pro and con, for tighter security. Lawyer Jim Stephenson, one of the people shot at in the 1986 fracas, noted the openness of the courthouse. "Because of that, you have all kinds of people wandering around in there all the time."[18] He and several other lawyers expressed the need for metal detectors and more armed personnel. Ironically, the county owned thirty-eight metal detectors at the time of the 1992 shooting, but they were used only at the request of judges.

Not all workers and people using the building favored metal detectors. They questioned the effectiveness of such devices compared to the time-consuming bottlenecks they would cause. In the end those demanding greater security prevailed. In 1993 some doors were closed to the public. Major entrances were outfitted with metal detectors and x-ray machines manned by security officers around the clock. Workers and visitors have adjusted to the arrangements, believing their increased safety far outweighs the slight inconvenience.

The Texas Supreme Court

Traditionally, the Texas Supreme Court meets in the state capital. History was made March 4, 1999, when for the first time the state supreme court justices heard cases in Fort Worth. A constitutional amendment was passed in 1997 that allowed the justices to hold court outside of Austin. The first year after the amendment they met at Baylor University in Waco. On March 3, 1999, they heard two cases involving open-records requests at Southern Methodist University's Underwood Law Library.

The following day, Texas Wesleyan School of Law hosted the Fort Worth event. Vice Dean Richard Gershon noted that holding court in different areas is an advantage to both the public and the lawyers. The public, especially students, benefit from observing actual pleadings. "Attorneys arguing the cases benefit by not having to travel to Austin," he said.[1]

Justices Greg Abbott, James Baker, Craig Enoch, Al Gonzales, Deborah Hankinson, Nathan Hecht, Harriet O'Neill, Priscilla Owen, and Chief Justice Thomas Phillips welcome the opportunity to move around the state and expose more people to the court process.

At the law school, a large classroom was converted into a court for the occasion. A stage, accessible by ramp to accommodate wheelchair-bound Justice Greg Abbott, was constructed. Tables, chairs, and microphones were arranged on the stage. Dean of Student Services Deborah Fathree coordinated the revisions.

Wesleyan law students drew lottery numbers for the coveted seats in the improvised courtroom. Many practicing attorneys and nine area high school students were in attendance. The nine high school students were given a tour of the law school and a briefing on what to expect. They were told no cellular phones, pagers, food, or cameras would be allowed in the courtroom. All were suitably dressed for the august occasion. "'This is the first time,' noted Fathree, 'that high school students have been invited to hear the Supreme Court.'"[2]

Two auditorium-style classrooms were outfitted with closed-circuit television and giant screens for the overflow crowd. First-year students and other spectators filled the rooms. Unlike the lucky ones who got seats in the courtroom, these students were informally dressed in jeans and sneakers, along with their backpacks.

Because one of the cases involved an insurance claim, two attorneys from a San Antonio insurance corporation were there. "We represent State Farm and have a similar case coming up, so we wanted to be here," one said.[3]

Shortly after 9:00 A.M. the court crier solemnly intoned "Oye, oye, God save the state of Texas and this honorable court. All rise." The nine black-robed justices entered and seated themselves at the tables on stage. Chief Justice Phillips made a few opening remarks and called the first case.

Being at the appellate level, the justices hear cases from lower courts. There are no witnesses, no jury, no testimony, and few visual aids. Reporter Linda Campbell, covering the historic visit, explained to her readers, "Because appellate courts focus on interpretations of law, the judges hear only from lawyers."[4] Each side had thirty minutes to convince the nine legal scholars of the validity of their clients' claims. Throughout the presentations the justices bombarded the attorneys with probing questions.

In the first presentation, justices heard disputation over how much money motorists can recover from their insurance companies when they hold both personal injury protection (PIP) and uninsured motorist policies. Plaintiff Jack Kidd had been paid $10,000 by Mid-Century Insurance Co. of Texas in actual damages under the (PIP) provision of his automobile policy. "A jury then awarded Kidd $13,000 more under his uninsured motorist provision, but Mid-Centruy balked at paying the full amount."[5] Mid-Century contended it had already paid Kidd $10,000 and only owed him $3,000 more.

In a similar case, Catherine Gerlich was paid $2,208 by Nationwide Mutual Insurance Co. under provisions of her PIP policy. Gerlich then settled for $3,500 from her uninsured motorist policy. But Nationwide argued they owed her only $1,291 because she had already received $2,208.

The motorists' representatives argued the insurance companies shouldn't be allowed to essentially take back money to which their clients were entitled by virtue of paying premiums for uninsured motorist coverage. Lawyers for the insurers argued against what they perceived to be double recovery. "No one has a right to come out ahead," said El Paso attorney Kurt Paxon, representing Mid-Century.[6]

"But didn't they pay extra for two types of coverage?" asked Judge Abbott.[7] He asked the insurance lawyers, "Why shouldn't they be able to collect if they paid separate premiums for the two coverage provisions?"[8]

Justice Hankinson asked several pointed questions on whether premiums are calculated to protect motorists from losing money if the insurance companies get to subtract PIP benefits from total payments.

"These aren't PIP benefits that are being paid. These are PIP advances that are being paid," San Antonio attorney Larry Zinn told the nine jurists, as he argued for his client, Gerlich.[9]

On more than one occasion the lawyers referred to case law to bolster their contentions, and at times they admitted they were not prepared to answer a judge's question about case law. After hearing from two attorneys for both sides, court was recessed for fifteen minutes.

Again, everyone stood as the justices filed in. Chief Justice Phillips again called the court into session. Arguments were heard concerning whether suits against Union Pacific Railroad Company in Texas must be filed in Harris County. Houston attorney Deborah Newman alleged the suits belonged in Harris County because that is where Union Pacific has its only principal office.

Lauren Melton, a Texas Wesleyan Law School graduate, spoke for six workers injured in Fort Worth and Beaumont. They wanted trials in the cities in which they lived and worked. She told the visiting justices both cities had officials who made significant and binding company decisions. This, in effect, proved that Union Pacific had principal offices in Fort Worth and Beaumont. For the workers to have to travel to Houston would place an unnecessary burden upon them, she said.

After hearing the arguments, the bailiff intoned, "Oye, oye, the Supreme Court of Texas is now adjourned." Rulings are not expected to be handed down for several months.

Some students who witnessed the rare event plan to study law; others saw it as a must-see opportunity. They gave it their enthusiastic approval. Jim Oldner, second-year law student, was impressed. "Both presentations were outstanding," he said. "The Court has a difficult job when the issues at question were as narrowly divided as these were."[10] Arlington Martin High School junior Safiya Porter said, "The questions the justices asked were amazing."[11]

Michael Crain, president of the Law School Student Bar Association, was pleased with the Supreme Court visit and the impact it would have on the school. "Their visit here, passing up the other venues they could have used in Fort Worth, gives credence to the fact that Texas Wesleyan University School of Law is on its way to becoming an established, world class law school."[12]

The judges in turn were impressed with Fort Worth. Justice Harriet O'Neill was pleased with the law school. "I had not been here," she said. "I am surprised at how nice the facilities are."[13]

Law School Dean Frank Walwer was as enthusiastic as the students. "I understand from the justices and others that they were very satisfied by the turnout," he told Texas Wesleyan *Rambler* reporter Scott Huber.[14] Walwer stressed the importance of the visit to law school students. "This provided an excellent opportunity for our students to be exposed to law practice at the highest judicial level in the state."[15]

Following the hearings, the Tarrant County Bar Association hosted a luncheon and presented the justices each with a Fort Worth souvenir—a Stetson hat from Luskey's Western Wear.

Texas Supreme Court justices visit Texas Wesleyan University School of Law and hear oral arguments March 4, 1999.

—Courtesy Texas Wesleyan University School of Law

The Frederick A. Cook
Oil Scandal Trial

A s a percentage, only a small number of trials involve the crime of murder, and those that do in no way resemble popular television dramas. In real life, lawyers don't deliver the culprit seconds before the closing commercial. They do spend hours and hours before the trial studying case law, interviewing witnesses and experts, and preparing their presentations to the judge or jury. While civil lawsuits far outnumber criminal ones, they usually don't get the publicity accorded a criminal trial. And few criminal trials that do not involve murder and mayhem receive extensive coverage. A trial that did was the case of *United States of America v. F. A. Cook, et al.*

The Ranger and Burkburnett oil strikes energized the Fort Worth community even more than the cattle drives and the coming of the railroad. Fortunes were made and lost in a day, and swindlers were a dime a dozen.

Oil first affected the city's growth in 1911. Roger and Diana Olien, in their book *Oil Promoters and Investors in the Jazz Age: Easy Money*, stated, "By mid-1918 Fort Worth showed many of the familiar signs of a community in the midst of an oil boom; all that was missing were the derricks and gushers."[1] An army of oil operators descended upon the city on the Trinity.

One such operator was Dr. Frederick Cook. A friend

described him as a man of average size with above average ability and tremendous faith in his fellow man. He was born in Sullivan County, New York, in 1865. His father, also a physician, died when the boy was five years old. His mother moved with her family of five children to Brooklyn. Times were hard for the widow who eked out a living working in the sweatshops.

"My boyhood was not happy," Cook wrote in his biography. "As a tiny child I was discontented, and from the early days of consciousness I felt the burden of two things which accompanied me through later life—an innate and abnormal desire for exploration, then the manifestation of my yearning, and the constant struggle to make ends meet, that sting of poverty which, while it tantalizes one with its horrid grind, sometimes drives men by reason of the strength developed ... to some extraordinary achievement."[2]

Psychological research also shows that for some, early deprivation leads to an attitude of always seeking more material goods as a hedge against recurring hard times. Perhaps both rationales applied to Cook.

He worked his way through medical school, and in the first year of his practice his wife Mary Elizabeth died in childbirth. Nor did the infant survive. Cook assuaged his grief by reading of travel and exploration. In 1901 he was employed by Robert E. Peary as surgeon and ethnologist for the North Pole expedition. Cook would maintain all his life that he, not Peary, was the first to reach the Pole.

After his return to the United States, for five years he traveled the country lecturing to support his claim. The National Geographic Society refuted his contention, and Peary won all the acclaim. Disheartened, Cook accepted the offer from a friend to investigate some oil leases in Wyoming.

In 1916 a man did not need a degree in geology to be knowledgeable about oil, Hugh Eames claimed in his book *Winner Lose All*. The early discoveries were made along creek beds and "oil men were students of creekology. They also employed oil smellers, fortune tellers, wiggle-stick operators, and persons with x-ray eyes," he said.[3] Cook, a medical doctor, became field supervisor for the New York Oil Company.

With partner Frank G. Curtis putting up the money, the

Cook Oil Company was formed with the doctor as president. It was moderately successful, but the really big money was being made in Texas. The explorer-turned-oil operator sold his stake in the company for $40,000 and headed south.

In Fort Worth thousands of men boarded the trains every morning and rode to the Ranger or Burkburnett fields. Tired, dirty, and occasionally richer, they poured back onto the trains for the return to the city. By 1919 when Cook arrived, "Fort Worth . . . was headquarters for some 2,000 independent oil companies, each of which based their operations on two facts that had become evident over the years: that the public purchased oil stock because it was hungry to get rich; and that most of those people who invested in oil and failed to profit would continue to invest."[4]

An investor might buy a one-eighth royalty in a drilling site, unaware that as many as 500,000 other investors might own shares in the same site. One couple, fifty years after the oil boom, bought a weekend retreat of three acres and a house, minus mineral rights, in the Ranger area. Legal records revealed those rights belonged to so many investors that the three acres looked like it had been divided into postage stamps.

But during the boom, people almost pleaded with operators to take their money. And Cook did. Of the 1,050 Texas oil companies organized in 1918 and 1919, only seven paid dividends. Cook hit upon a way to make money from the ones coming up with dry holes.

Cook formed the Petroleum Producers Association in March of 1922 and named himself as president and sole trustee. Rather than drilling for oil, which cost from $35,000 to $40,000 per well, Cook prospered by merging small, mostly insolvent companies with the PPA.

A November 1922 *Fort Worth Press* story, headlined "Ha! They'll Not Beat 'Doc' Out of THIS Discovery!" gave an example of Cook's merger offering. Evidently he was not pleased with it and later accounts, because the following February he sued for $1,000,000 in damages, claiming he had been libeled. The petition characterized Dr. Cook "as a 'good, true, honest and respectable citizen.'" He objected to the *Press* article referring to him "as 'a promoter of gush and hot air, promoter of falsehoods and misrepresentations, promoter of trickery and fraud'. . . ."⁵

A letter introduced into evidence at Cook's mail fraud trial shows how he operated. Addressed to W. R. Beach, holder of stock in the Middle Georgia Oil and Gas Company, and written by one of Cook's employees, it reads in part:

> The letter-documents herewith enclosed carry a double message of great importance to you. For some time you have been awaiting reports from your company, but during the passing months all business has undergone periods of hardships. For this reason, your company has had little to report. Perhaps you have not understood the long silence, but in cooperation with others I have worked for your interest and for your ultimate profit. [For the next several paragraphs he expounds on the downturn.]
>
> . . . I have arranged for you to enter the Petroleum Producer's Association, and I feel assured that when you convert your stock into association shares as hereinafter provided, your original investment will be well placed, and thereafter you will be in a position for the double profit always possible in oil. [The letter then extols the expertise of Cook, identified as a "petroleum technologist."]
>
> The Directing Board is headed by E. A. Reilly, who drilled the famous Trapshooter wells in Kansas. He is regarded as the most successful independent oil operator in the United States. Reilly has been one of the largest dividend payers of all time. . . .
>
> Petroleum Producers Association, therefore, which you enter by the agreement herein outlined, has acquired great values from merging companies. . . . The Association has an income from nearly one hundred wells already drilled, which is equal to a hearty dividend of 25% on all stock sold. . . . We urge upon you the importance of sending in your stock certificates with the remittance required promptly.⁶

The remittance asked for was to buy shares of PPA at a price above the par value, plus the surrender of shares in Middle Georgia Oil and Gas. The letter to Beach was signed by O. L. Ray. Ray later plea bargained and testified for the state in exchange for a lighter sentence.

Cook sent thousands of letters such as the one above to

stockholders in small oil operations. "It took him a mere 12 months to merge with 413 companies, placing them all under one name, Petroleum Producers Association."[7] So successful was he that his company occupied an entire floor of the Farmers and Merchants Building in downtown Fort Worth. It appeared he would fulfill his childhood dreams of never being poor again.

But on July 10, 1923, Cook and twenty-five employees were indicted by a federal grand jury for mail fraud. The indictments resulted from the Post Office's extensive investigation launched in August 1922. Local federal attorney Henry Zweifel took the mass of evidence to the grand jury in April 1923. After a week of deliberation, it returned indictments against ninety-two individuals, including a former Tarrant County attorney, a former sheriff, and fourteen separate companies. Petroleum Producers Association was one of them. Regarding Cook and his associates, the federal indictments charged one count of misuse of the mails to defraud and eleven specific instances of ways in which the frauds were carried out.

> The Grand Jurors of the United States of America, duly impanelled, sworn and charged to inquire into and true presentment make of crimes and offenses within and for the body of the Fort Worth Division of the Northern District of Texas, upon their oaths present, that FREDERICK A. COOK . . . [others listed] hereinafter designated and referred to as the defendants, . . . had devised and had intended to devise a scheme and artifice to defraud and to obtain money and property by means of false and fraudulent pretenses, representations and promises from Mrs. William F. Poettig, . . . [others listed].[8]

The grand jury charged that Cook and his associates had organized an oil promotion scheme "under the guise and form of a trust estate to be known as Petroleum Producers Association, giving to the defendants the entire control of the assets, business, operations, and policies of the same without regard to the other persons who would be induced to purchase an interest called shares or units in said Petroleum Producers Association as hereinafter set forth."[9]

The report went on to say, "And the said defendants planned and schemed to promote and operate the said

Petroleum Producers Association as a so-called merger concern. . . . Some of such companies were entirely defunct and without assets of any sort, and others were still operating although insolvent while still others were solvent, going concerns being operated at a profit. It was part of the scheme of the said defendants that they would from time to time fraudulently procure lists of stockholders of said companies, such stockholders being among the persons to be defrauded, and thereupon would falsely announce and advertise mergers . . . [with Petroleum Producers Association]."[10] W. R. Beach, cited above, was one such stockholder.

The report noted two ways in which Cook perpetrated the fraud. First he would convince shareholders to exchange shares in their oil company plus extra investments for shares in Petroleum Producers Association. Those shareholders were assured the only way to redeem their investments was to merge. Cook and his associates also sold shares or units in PPA outright.

The indictment listed other illegal practices, such as advertising "that the said Petroleum Producers Association was exceedingly successful as an oil producing company and had an income from producing wells equal to a yearly dividend of 25% of all outstanding stock, . . . [and had] over one hundred wells pouring money into the dividend account."[11]

Cook and his employees claimed "dividends were as safe as any cash distribution can be in any investment; Whereas, in truth and in fact, as the defendants then and there well knew, the said [PPA] did not at the time the said representations were made, or at anytime, have an income from producing wells . . . nor any net earnings whatever; . . . the said dividends at the said rate were not as safe as any cash . . . but on the contrary were unsafe because there were no funds out of which dividends could be legitimately paid."[12]

The twelve-count indictment also refuted the PPA's claims to having a geologist on its payroll; that Cook was an experienced, successful oil explorer; that one well was producing 25,000 barrels a day; and $2.00 shares could go up to $40.00 in sixty to ninety days.

On April 3, 1923, Cook surrendered at the Federal Building. He entered a plea of not guilty and was released on $25,000 bond. In July Cook was also indicted by a grand jury sitting in Cleveland, Ohio, on basically the same charges, but his trial would be in Fort Worth.

Federal attorney Zweifel sought as much publicity as he could generate, hoping to warn future investors to beware. He told reporters the scams involved $200 million, taken from over two million victims. Knowing local federal Judge James C. Wilson to be lenient, Zweifel filed so many cases it became necessary to call in an additional judge. In Washington Chief Justice William Howard Taft sent John M. Killits to help with the overload.

This was exactly what Zweifel hoped for, and he filed the most egregious cases, including the PPA, in visiting Judge Killits' court. Killits was a man of sterling reputation and vast judicial experience in fraud cases. Moreover, the judge knew something about the oil industry as he was a disappointed investor in several dry hole companies. "It is also likely that he was keenly interested in Cook's merger scheme; during the trial he received notice that one of the companies in which he invested had been merged."[13]

Zweifel was joined by John S. Pratt and Sylvester Rush, both special assistants of the United States attorney general. Former Senator Joseph W. Bailey and the firm of Greathouse and Wade appeared as counsel for the defendant.

On October 14, 1923, opening day of the trial, spectators observed an imposing array of principal characters in the drama. Cook, dressed in a well-cut dark suit and carrying an expensive-looking briefcase, looked like one of the lawyers, except for one feature. In a fashion period long past the 1870s and long before the 1970s, he wore his stringy hair shoulder length.

Zweifel—short, stocky, and wiry-haired—looked like the oil field worker he once was, except now he wore a conservative business suit. But it was Bailey who stole the show.

A congressman in 1890, he was elected to the Senate ten years later. "Bailey specialized in dramatic poses, parliamentary maneuvers, and eloquent rhetoric, making effective use of his melodious voice, tall frame, and handsome face."[14] Sure of himself, he looked the part of a senator in his long frock coat and broad-brimmed hat. He saw the Cook trial, with its attendant publicity, as his ticket back to the center stage he had enjoyed as a politician.

Seven defendants pleaded guilty of using the mails to defraud. That left fourteen, the main one being Cook.

The trial was identified as No. 2273

IN THE DISTRICT COURT OF THE UNITED STATES
FOR THE NORTHERN DISTRICT OF TEXAS
FORT WORTH DIVISION
UNITED STATES OF AMERICA
V
FREDERICK A. COOK *ET AL.*

The first action by Bailey was a bill of exceptions. Defined as "a formal statement in writing of the objections or exceptions taken by a party . . . the object being to put the controverted rulings or decisions upon the record for the information of the appellate court," Bailey used it as a defensive tactic.[15] Faced with the mountain of evidence against his client, his strategy was to object at every turn and pave the way for an appeal.

Killits's handwritten response rejected the bill of exception, noting, "[it] is found wholly insufficient to carry up all this necessary part of the record . . . wherefore the court declines to sign and seal this [handwriting illegible]. May 7, 1924, John M. Killits, Judge."[16] Before the cases and all appeals were over, thousands of pages of testimony and legal proceedings would document the case against Cook, as well as the many clashes between Bailey and Killits.

Henry Zweifel knew that jurors related better to people than to dry facts and figures understandable only to accountants. Over defense attorney Bailey's objections, Zweifel placed sixty-six-year-old Mrs. Mary Phillips on the stand. The Civil War veteran's widow limped to the witness box and was sworn in. "I am living in poverty. It's the God's truth. I told Dr. Cook that I took the rugs off the floor to buy oil stock and that I had sent him all the money that I could. It seemed I couldn't satisfy him, as he kept asking for more money."[17] At one point in her testimony she broke down in tears, and Judge Killits had to call for a brief adjournment. "After this delay, she concluded her testimony, left the stand, and berated Cook before a startled judge and sympathetic jury."[18]

What followed was an example of the wrangling between the defense and the Court. Senator Bailey objected, declaring letters to Mrs. Phillips and others were mimeographed and not sent directly by Dr. Cook, and their introduction by the government was merely to overwhelm the jury. Killits responded that the government did not send out the letters, to which Bailey quipped, "Well, the government seems to be the only ones that made any money out of it—through postage."

"That's pure buncombe," replied the court.[19] Judge Killits also sharply reprimanded Bailey for not facing him when addressing the Court. And so it went for the length of the trial.

The last witness for the prosecution, expert bank accountant of the Department of Justice, H. B. Matheny, testified his examination of the books of PPA revealed big operating losses. He found an operating deficit of $306,360; total assets were $145,641, and total liabilities $452,360. "The total income from oil production and royalties," he said, ". . . was but $14,468 and the bank balance on January 31 of this year [1923] was only $5,660."[20]

Matheney insisted accounting practices required the listing of outstanding stock as a liability. Bailey insisted just as fervently that Cook's method of counting stock as an asset was correct. The dispute touched off a legal wrangle that must have left the jurors with numbers swimming in their heads. Forty-three pages of transcript involved the differences in accounting practices and the "expertness" of experts.

Prosecutor John Pratt questioned Frederick Cook on recross examination regarding how the shares of Double Head Oil Company were listed on the PPA's books.

> Q. Dr. Cook, how much of the stock of the Double Head Oil Company was transferred to your company?
> A. I don't know.
> Q. Whatever was transferred should also be added to the cost of those properties, should it not?
> MR. BAILEY: If your Honor please, in the first place that is a pure calculation, and not based on the fact at all, not based upon

the plan of organization, because the stock exchanged was stock exchanged for a stock exchange, and not for the property.

THE COURT: Senator, stock issued, becomes the liability of the corporation or organization issuing it.

MR. BAILEY: No, sir, no stock was ever a liability. A liability is a promise to pay. A stock is merely a right of the holder to participate in whatever is left after all the debts are paid.

THE COURT: Then if a company is merged, having in this peculiar way here, having an amount of property, and that property comes in, and stock is issued to the merging stockholders, the company acquiring it gets it for nothing?

MR. BAILEY: If Your Honor please, I am not clear, or Your Honor has misconceived the plan. . . .[21]

Much later in the same line of questioning, Pratt asked if "The stock issued by you to the Double Head Oil stockholders in exchange for their stock should be added to the cost of this property, the cost to you of this property? Isn't that a fact?"[22]

Defense attorney Bailey objected; Judge Killits told Cook to answer the question. More wrangling, objections, and counterobjections, and the question was never answered. Pratt moved on to the matter of financial statements.

Q. And in various corporations and organizations with which you have been connected, you have from time to time made financial statements, haven't you?

A. Possibly—usually I was not in the financial department.

Q. If you ever made any financial statement in connection with any corporation that you were associated with, was there ever a financial statement that did not carry the stock outstanding as a liability?

A. I don't remember.

Q. Do you know how much of the Double Head stock transferred to your company?

A. No.

Q. Did you ever keep any record in your organization—your accounting department, of the amount of the stock that the Double Head transferred?

A. We have.

Q. You have a record?

A. We have a specific record of every transaction, but we have not figured it up yet.[23]

Further probing revealed that the PPA did not have records in a form that would show at a glance how many shares of any of a hundred or so companies were involved in the mergers. Cook stated it would take as long as two weeks to go over every transaction to get the information the government asked for. Senator Bailey noted that the prosecution, in the person of Mr. Matheney, had examined the books. The next side argument was on the usefulness of accounting experts' opinions as to how a company should keep its financial records.

Concerning bringing the PPA's books to court, Bailey acknowledged there was not a tabulation.

> THE COURT: But, Senator, how could they possibly keep the books if they did not know how much stock obligation they had?
>
> MR. BAILEY: They could easily know. I won't say "easily"— I would have said "easily" until I heard the Government expert say that it would take him two weeks. I don't know how many— one transfer might include 100 shares, and another 10 shares, and another 1000 shares—no telling how many.
>
> THE COURT: If there was a bona fide expectation of paying dividends, how did they know how much to pay unless they had a stock ledger?[24]

Bailey explained it was difficult, and that was why they went to quarterly payouts instead of monthly ones.

Prosecutor Pratt interjected, "I want this record to show . . . that the Petroleum Producers Association kept no record showing the amount of stock transferred from these various so-called merging companies, so that therefore they could not take into account in figuring profits, the amount of stock transferred."[25]

Dr. Cook denied responsibility for the letters sent to Beach, Phillips, and others. He admitted he wrote O.K. on the draft copies, but explained the approval was to use the office mimeograph machine.

The judge would have none of it. "He [Cook] is responsible for that sent out by subordinates and for their statements of facts. There can be no question about that, and this will be the court's charge. The O.K. Dr. Cook placed on the letters does not permit him to escape the responsibility."[26]

After a total of fifteen hours on the stand, Cook was allowed to step down. The physician/explorer/oil operator was not without his supporters. One attorney sagely remarked there are two sides to every trial—that is why we have prosecutors and defense attorneys.

In his defense, biographer Howard S. Abramson forcefully argued that Cook's troubles resulted from a conspiracy by Robert Peary's supporters. Citing the oil operator's success at attracting stockholder-investors, "Cook was to pay once again for his audacity in trying to claim 'Peary's Pole.' . . . Herbert S. Houston, a publisher who had been a staunch supporter of Peary and was then the head of a group called the National Vigilance Committee, which purported to be a 'Better Business Bureau' in New York, charged that the Petroleum Producers Association was 'a gigantic reloading scheme.'"[27] Houston, according to Abramson, was a good friend of Herbert L. Bridgeman, "the man who had played such a critical role in the Peary cabal. Thus, Peary may have been dead, but his gang—and its campaign against Cook—was alive and well," he concluded. [28]

Abramson noted that President Warren G. Harding needed a scapegoat to gloss over the irregularities of the Teapot Dome scandal and had ordered federal prosecutors to conduct a witch hunt into Texas oil operations. Believing the government's case to be extremely weak, Abramson wrote, "These weaknesses in their case forced the government to pursue Cook under mail-fraud statutes because it was unable to attack him directly for allegedly bilking the investors."[29]

Another author who believed in Cook's innocence was Hugh Eames. In his book *Winner Lose All* he wrote, "It is contended here that Cook . . . was an honest man who had exposed himself to the hazards of an extremely speculative industry during a period of great optimism."[30] He further argued the whole case was built on "intent" and believed the government did not prove that Cook intended to defraud investors in the PPA. He cited as proof the fact that Cook put his own money into the venture and took no money out for himself. To bolster his contention, Eames quoted from the trial transcript.

Q. Dr. Cook, what was the first piece of property acquired by the Petroleum Producers Association?

A. The first piece. . . was a block of 121 acres in La Salle County, Texas.

Q. From whom did your company acquire that?

A. From myself.

Q. They did not pay for it?

A. They did not pay me anything for it.

Q. Did you receive anything from the company for it?

A. I received nothing and asked nothing.[31]

But Eames failed to point out that Cook was the owner and sole trustee of the PPA, and thus had merely transferred the property to another entity which he owned.

Concerning the solvency of the PPA, testimony showed that at the time of the trial, Cook was drilling a well at Corsicana and elsewhere. "It would appear, therefore, that PPA was very close to bringing in a gusher that would have enabled Cook to fulfill the statements made in the company's promotional letters."[32]

On Saturday, November 17 the testimony was heated as Senator Bailey called United States District Attorney Henry Zweifel to the stand. Questioned about promises of leniency for those who would turn against Dr. Cook, Zweifel emphatically denied assurances in exchange for testimony.

Yet another verbal confrontation erupted between Bailey and Judge Killits, but finally both sides rested. The following Monday Judge Killits delivered his charge to the jury. After two days of deliberation, the verdict was rendered on Wednesday at 2:10 P.M. "Dr. Frederick A. Cook, internationally known Arctic explorer, was found guilty on 12 counts of using the United States mails to defraud."[33]

The motion to dismiss was overruled, and on appeal Cook's fourteen-year sentence was upheld after years of legal maneuvering. He was sentenced to Leavenworth, where he maintained his innocence. Beach and Phillips believed him guilty; Abramson and Eames believed him not guilty. Only Cook knew for sure who was right.

The J. Frank Norris
Murder Trial

J. Frank Norris fervently believed God used him to denounce the wrongs of others, and to prove an ecclesiastical point he was not above doing wrong himself. To the casual observer it seemed as if Baptist preacher John Franklyn Norris spent almost as much time in the courthouse as he did in the church house. During his long and turbulent career he was indicted for torching his own church and once for shooting an unarmed man. Biographer Barry Hankins wrote, "While Norris's enemies often charged that he had no character, few have doubted that he was one."[1] His obsession with being in the center of controversy, mostly of his own concoction, made him the most famous, or infamous, Fort Worth preacher of the first half of the twentieth century.

Frank, as he referred to himself, was born September 18, 1877, to an alcoholic father and a devoutly religious mother. He grew up in Hubbard City, Texas, a small town thirty miles from Waco.

When Frank was thirteen years old, an enemy of his father opened fire on the elder Norris, then turned the weapon on the boy, shooting him three times. Warner Norris suffered minor injuries, but his son was not so fortunate. Frank was in critical condition for several days and later developed gangrene and inflammatory rheumatism. It took three years for him to regain his health.

At the age of twenty he felt the call to ministry and pastored small churches while attending Baylor University. Even at that early stage in his career he relished tweaking the beard of authority figures. During chapel some students smuggled a dog into the hall. When the animal's howls disrupted the service, the university president became so enraged he threw the dog out a window. The man later apologized for his loss of control, but Norris would not let the matter drop. He led a student demonstration and reported the incident to the Society for the Prevention of Cruelty to Animals and to the university trustees. The uproar was so great that the president was forced to resign.

Norris obtained his bachelor's degree from Baylor in 1903 and two years later graduated at the top of his class from Southern Baptist Seminary in Louisville, Kentucky. Back in Texas, he pastored for the next five years the McKinney Avenue Baptist Church in Dallas, and owned and edited the *Baptist Standard*. It was as a publisher that he tasted the glory of public confrontation. It would change his life.

As editor he lobbied against racetrack gambling with such vigor that when the state legislature outlawed the amusement, Norris was invited to attend the governor's signing ceremony. For the next forty years he craved the spotlight like addicts crave their next fix.

Fort Worth's First Baptist Church was built in 1876 and originally located on Jennings Street. Later a rock structure was built at Third and Taylor. In 1909 he accepted the call to that congregation. A powerhouse in the Southern Baptist Convention, it was the home church of many of the city's richest families. But being a dispassionate preacher, even to a flock of millionaires and movers and shakers, did not scratch his itch for fame. He embarked upon policies and a preaching style that pushed the more sedate congregants away. In their place came droves of what he called "the little people."

He became a populist preacher. Each Sunday's sermon seemed more outlandish than the last, and the people loved it. Not only was he preaching against the biblical Devil, he maintained the city fathers were in cahoots with the forked-tailed rascal. In January 1912 he accused Mayor W. D. "Bill" Davis of misappropriating city funds. The mayor lashed back with threats. Saying Norris was a "fanatical outcast, [not] worth killing with a dollar ninety-eight-cent pistol," he urged the men of the city to act. "If there are fifty red-blooded men in town, a preacher will be hanging from a lamp post before daylight."[2] No vigilante justice took place, and Norris reveled in the publicity the tiff caused.

That same month the first of two fires damaged the First Baptist Church. The second fire, on February 5, destroyed the building. Norris's home at 810 W. Fifth Street suffered some fire damage as well.

"To convince the public that he was the object of a conspiracy, Norris produced threatening letters he claimed to have received before the fires."[3] Mayor Davis hired a private detective to investigate and on March 1 a grand jury indicted Norris for perjury in connection with the letters. The next day another fire was discovered at Norris's home. Skeptics questioned how the fire could spread as much as it did without arousing the family or awakening the night watchman. Their questions were answered March 28, 1912, when Norris was indicted for arson. He was charged with setting fire to the church and his home.

In a three-week trial in April, he was acquitted on the perjury account. The arson trial was not held until January 1914. The judge on at least four occasions stated his belief in Norris's innocence. The prosecution tried unsuccessfully to have the judge recuse himself. When asked about an appeal in the case of conviction the judge said, "That matter will not come up. There will not be a conviction."[4] The judge was right. There was no conviction.

Norris and his followers were ecstatic. His supporters "raised the rafters" singing hymns in the courtroom. Once again he had gone up against the politically powerful and won. Norris believed himself to be a modern David, slaying the Goliaths he saw as opposed to him and the "little people." But like King David, whose absolute power led him to sin before God, Norris was becoming totally autocratic. G. B. Vick, a one-time associate, reluctantly concluded "that Norris was a dictator who had to control all facets of everything with which he was involved."[5]

A year after the fire, a new church was erected at Fourth and Throckmorton. Believed to have the largest sanctuary in the county, it was 200 feet long, 100 feet wide, with the total space of the church being 32,000 square feet. It housed the flock until it too was destroyed by fire in 1928. Norris led in the rebuilding, this time at Fourth and Taylor.

In his most serious escapade, Norris, in his gravely voice, railed against another mayor, H. C. Meacham. The year was 1926, and Norris was openly contemptuous of Catholics. Meacham was Catholic. In a sermon the preacher alleged the mayor was trying to

The Reverend J. Frank Norris.
—Photo courtesy UTA
Special Collections Library

enrich a Catholic church and school at the city's expense. He maintained Meacham overvalued a piece of land that the city bought from St. Ignatius School. Moreover he, the mayor, was planning to re-route traffic to enhance his department store business.

The following week Norris's newsletter the *Searchlight* headlined the firing of six church members by the Roman Catholic manager of Meacham's Dry Goods Company. In an emotional

Sunday morning testimony, the fired workers related how they were told to choose between their jobs and their church. They chose to remain at First Baptist.

Norris characterized city manager H. B. Carr as the "missing link" and noted that Meacham was not "fit to be mayor of a hog pen."[6] This occurred on July 11.

The next Saturday Dexter Elliot Chipps, a friend and supporter of the mayor, visited Norris at the church. Trial transcripts show that several people were at the church, but Norris and the wealthy lumberman were alone in his office when shots rang out. Norris admitted shooting Chipps, claiming self-defense.

Because of the intense publicity, the January 1927 trial was moved to Austin. Balding, white-mustached Judge James Hamilton presided; attorneys Marvin Simpson and Dayton Moses defended Norris. Tarrant County District Attorney Jesse E. Martin (TCU Law School class of 1918) prosecuted for the state. He was joined by W. R. McLean, John Shelton, Walter Scott, and Samuel Sayers as special prosecutors. The latter four had been engaged by Mayor Meacham. Travis County District Attorney D. A. Moore also aided in the trial.

Three hundred fifty-one potential jurors were called. The defense struck Catholics since Norris's views toward the Roman Catholic Church were well-known. The prosecution refused to seat Ku Klux Klansmen as they believed the defendant had sympathizers in that group. The state required potential jurors to support the death penalty, and the other side sounded out jurors on the concept of "apparent danger" self-defense. Martin and his team also wanted jurors who would not hold ministers of the Gospel in higher regard than laymen when considering testimony. Jury selection was a tedious process, but finally on January 14 the trial was ready to begin.

Spectators lined the corridors waiting for the courtroom to open. Gray-haired men and women with small children jostled each other in their headlong dash to get the best viewing spots. Some 150 of them brought sack lunches so as not to lose their seats by going out to lunch. "The courtroom was 'sold out' by 9:15 A.M.," Frank Evans, the *Fort Worth Star-Telegram* Austin correspondent reported.[7] There were so many called to testify that the regular holding room proved too small, and bailiffs converted a Civil District Courtroom into the witness room.

The state took one day to present to the jury evidence that Norris fired three bullets into Chipps, killing him instantly. "D. E. Chipps [was] shot once below the heart and twice in the right side of the chest near the shoulder with a .38 caliber pistol."[8] They stressed that had the man come with intent to harm, he would have been armed. Scoffing at the notion of shooting an unarmed man as an act of self-defense, they accused Norris of welcoming the opportunity to rid himself of an enemy.

The defense called several who were members of Norris's congregation. Witnesses used a model replica of the church office area to show where they were at the time of the shooting. None actually saw the shooting, but they testified to seeing an angry Chipps burst into Norris's office.

Mrs. Lorene Rains, stenographer for First Baptist, testified to seeing a man leaning over the body. Defense attorneys sought to establish the possibility that this unnamed person might have been one of Meacham's men removing Chipps's gun. Prosecutors pointed out that Chipps was not known to carry a gun, did not have, and had never owned one.

Jane Hartwell, Norris's private secretary, in sworn testimony to the Tarrant County grand jury told of "hearing Chipps say 'I am going to kill you.' He ran his hand into his big pocket and pulled out a gun. Dr. Norris who was standing by his desk fired several shots first. Chipps fell to the floor of the office."[9] In light of police not finding a gun on the victim, Miss Hartwell realized she was mistaken in the confusion of the episode.

The important testimony of L. H. Nutt, bank auditor and trustee of First Baptist Church, and Jane Hartwell, despite her earlier version of the shooting, bolstered the minister's recounting of the event.

Dr. O. R. Grogan, in testifying to his credentials, stated he was a graduate of the old Fort Worth University Medical School. He had been in practice for twelve years, was a member of First Baptist, and was the defendant's physician. Dr. Grogan told the jury of twelve men that Norris suffered from neuritis.

Q. Now, I am not a physician and these gentlemen on the

jury are not. Just state what the effect of neuritis would be on a human being.

A. Well, the condition of neuritis, as the term applies, is an inflammation of the nerves. . . . (It) has a tendency to make a man rather nervous. . . . [He went on to explain that a person with such a condition would have intermittent pains such as one would suffer with appendicitis. Then he was asked about any effect upon one's strength.] It generally keeps a man in somewhat of a rundown condition. . . .[10]

Thus the defense established that Norris was no physical match for the burly Chipps.

Prosecutors, in rebutting the testimony of defense witnesses, pointed out to the jury the absence of objectivity concerning their pastor. The jury was not swayed.

The most riveting witness was Norris himself. The last to be called, his emotions ranged from frowning and biting his lip to a teary-eyed recitation on the stand.

Questioned by defense attorneys, he answered questions about his education and ministry. He acknowledged knowing Meacham in an adversarial position since 1920, but maintained he did not know D. E. Chipps. Norris and his attorneys more than once attempted to introduce the idea that a Meacham/Chipps conspiracy was trying to undermine his effectiveness as a spokesman on ethical lapses in city government.

As a witness Norris repeatedly answered questions to which the state objected. For example, defense attorney Moses instructed his client: "Dr. Norris, don't answer this until they have time to make an objection, if they so desire. Did you have a visit from H. C. Meacham shortly before the death of D. E. Chipps?

"A. Yes, sir."

Prosecutor Martin interjected, "I asked you not to answer that until I had time to object. Didn't you understand that?"

Defense attorney Simpson jumped into the argument, "Counsel has no right—"

Martin responded, "I want to object to this witness answering the question, and I want to further object to the question as to what any conversation he might have had with H. C. Meacham or anyone else, until some connection is shown. It is irrelevant and immaterial."

The Court ruled, "Objection sustained to that at this time."[11] After several such forays into the relationship between Norris and Meacham, Judge Hamilton ordered the jury to disregard any reference to a conspiracy, but the seed had already been planted.

Leading up to questioning about the shooting, the defense introduced evidence that Chipps had a reputation for violence. Norris testified that Chipps threatened him in a telephone call the afternoon of the killing.

> Q. Now, go ahead, Doctor, and tell the court and jury that conversation as best you remember it, from beginning to end; and what you did during the time of the conversation, if anything.
>
> A. I said, "Hello," and a woman's voice answered back . . . and said "Hello, Dr. Norris." There was a pause and a man's voice came on the line and said "Hello." I answered back "Hello, this is Dr. Norris," and then I couldn't understand what the other party was saying. I said "Who is this? . . . What do you want?" . . . then I heard this in a louder voice. In words and substance like this: "We are coming over there to settle with you on that sermon," and when I asked, "Who is this?" and a voice came back, "It don't matter—" Shall I repeat it?
>
> Q. Yes, sir, the conversation as you remember it.
>
> A. (Witness continuing) "I am not going to stand it any longer. I am coming over there to kill you, you __ __ __ __."[12]

In answer to later questioning, Norris related how the man came to his office and was asked to leave.

> Q. What did you say, Doctor?
>
> A. I looked at him and saw he was so mad. I said, "I don't want any trouble with you. . . . There is the door, and I want you to go."[13]

Norris further testified that Chipps walked toward the door and went out to the anteroom, then turned to face him. "Standing before the jury, Rev. Mr. Norris described how Chipps placed his hand near his right hip pocket just before the shots were fired."[14]

> Q. What did you think he was about to do?

A. I thought he was about to kill me.[15]
Moses—Would you have on that occasion killed him had you not believed your life was in danger?
A. I would not—I didn't want to kill him.[16]

Only a white handkerchief was found in Chipps's hip pocket. In closing arguments the state contended the position of the body, lying in the anteroom just outside the pastor's study, indicated Chipps was leaving, but turned around in response to Norris calling his name. It was at that time he was fatally wounded. McLean hammered away on the vague testimony of Norris's witnesses, implying they were imprecise because they really hadn't witnessed Chipps threatening their preacher.

Moses and Simpson reiterated that Norris feared for his life, had been threatened, and basic self preservation motivated his actions.

The jury believed their argument. Judge Hamilton finished reading the charge to the jury at 9:25 A.M. Final arguments lasted until 10:00 P.M. The jury deliberated less than an hour. Their first ballot was unanimous for acquittal.

When the district clerk announced the "not guilty" verdict, clapping broke out in the courtroom. "Norris showed no emotion until he made his way to . . . Simpson. Then he sobbed aloud and hugged the lawyer," according to the *Star-Telegram* story of the acquittal.[17] Upon his arrival back in Fort Worth, Norris participated in a hurriedly called service at the church. Hundreds of wellwishers gathered for what the chairman of the board of deacons called "Not a celebration, but a time of thanksgiving to Almighty God for His marvelous deliverance."[18]

Norris was still the object of controversy, and suspicions about him were aroused just two years later. On January 12, 1929, it was reported, "The First Baptist Church burned down this morning while Pastor J. Frank Norris was away. Investigation for incendiarism is being made, since three tubs and a jug partly filled with gasoline were found in the ruins of the structure. The loss is to be $200,000."[19]

Investigators failed to determine the cause of the blaze. One possibility was combustion from a pile of oily rags which had been allowed to collect in the basement. "Mrs. Rains believed it could possibly have been caused by a carelessly thrown cigarette from one of the hobos who frequently were permitted to sleep in the church basement."[20] Whatever the cause, charges were never filed, and a still bigger church was built.

Norris spent the next twenty-five years fighting the Southern Baptist Convention, believing that body was straying from its fundamentalist roots. He pastored Temple Baptist Church in Detroit as well as First Baptist in Fort Worth. He also established a Bible college and operated a radio station. Homer G. Ritchie, Norris's successor at First Baptist, chronicled the life of his mentor in *The Life and Legend of J. Frank Norris, The Fighting Parson*. J. Frank Norris retired from the battlefield in 1951 and died a year later at the age of seventy-four.

The Legacy of Oil Money

If one asked the man on the street in Vernon, Texas, the main employer in his city, the answer well could be "The Waggoner Estate." In 1991 it was estimated that the estate, directly and indirectly, provided an annual three million dollar payroll for the wind-swept city of 12,000 people. If one asked estate lawyers the most complicated civil litigation of the twentieth century, the answer well could be "The Waggoner Estate." Established in 1923, with W. T. Waggoner as the first trustee, seventy-five years later the Forty-sixth District Court was still hearing arguments involving the heirs.

Wilbarger County historians claim, "The roots of the W. T. Waggoner Estate date back to 1828 in Lincoln County, Tennessee, where Daniel Waggoner was born and was one of the eight children of Solomon and Elizabeth Waggoner."[1]

Solomon moved his family to Hopkins County, Texas, where he died when Daniel was twenty-one years old.

Dan, as he was known, established a 15,000-acre ranch in Wise County. In 1870 he and his eighteen-year-old son, William Thomas (W. T.), drove a herd of less than 300 head to Kansas City. There Dan sold the cattle and used the money to buy land at a dollar an acre near Wichita Falls. These drives continued until 1882, with the money from cattle sales going toward buying more land.

W. T. Waggoner expanded his holdings until the 1881 figure stood at 510,000 acres, spread across most of two Northwest Texas counties and parts of four others. Some sources say 600,000 acres, and whichever figure is used, the Waggoner Estate is roughly two-thirds the size of the state of Rhode Island. He called his main headquarters the Zacaweista Ranch. The backward Three-D brand became one of the best known in the state.

W. T. always considered himself a cattleman, but it was oil that propelled his fortune into the stratosphere and set the stage for lengthy and complex litigation. Stories abound concerning his disgust at finding oil when digging for wells to water his cattle. "Oil, oil, what do I want with damn oil? I'm looking for water. That's what my cattle need."[2] That was in 1903. It took five years for the rich oil pocket to be put into full production.

He developed the Electra oil field and soon became a millionaire. It was Will Rogers' exaggeration to say "Waggoner had one oil well per head of cattle, but by 1928 nineteen different companies had producing wells on the ranch."[3] Later Waggoner moved to Fort Worth and built a skyscraper which is still occupied today.

To understand the complex litigation, it is necessary to be familiar with the Waggoner family tree. W. T. (8/1/1852-12/11/1934) married Ella Halsell (3/27/1859-5/17/1959). They had five children, but two did not live past childhood. Dan E., born in 1879, died two years later. Willie Tom was born in 1885 and died in 1887.

Electra (hereinafter referred to as Electra I) was born January 15, 1882. She married three times and had two children by her first husband, A. B. Wharton, Sr. Their older son was Tom Waggoner Wharton (10/3/1903-10/8/1928). He married eight times, but had no children. Electra I and Wharton Sr.'s son, A. B. Wharton, Jr. (8/8/1909-5/28/1963) married four times and had one biological son and one adopted daughter. Electra I took back her maiden name after divorcing her third husband, James A. Gilmore. She died November 26, 1925. Her trust would be the basis of a lengthy court battle forty years later.

Guy Leslie Waggoner, W. T. and Ella's first son to live to be an adult, was born September 21, 1883. He married Katherine Brown and they had one son, W. T. Waggoner, Jr. Guy Leslie then married Lucille Elliott, and they were the parents of Guy L. Waggoner, Jr. Guy Sr. again married Katherine Brown, then five other women. There were no children from these later marriages.

E. Paul Waggoner (4/9/1899-3/3/67), the other son who lived to adulthood, married Helen Buck. Their daughter was named for her aunt and is referred to here as Electra II.

In 1910 W. T.'s children's Christmas stockings held more than trinkets. He divided his ranch, cattle, and horses among them. The gifts were valued at $2 million each. Electra I registered a circle on the hipbone as her brand, and she also got the Zacaweista Headquarters. Guy L. headquartered at the Four Corners Ranch. His brand was a backward Two-D. Paul's brand was a heart.

"The three divisions were operated as separate units until 1923 when by mutual agreement the three merged and became the Waggoner Estate Ranch."[4] Intended to last for twenty years, in 1934 it was extended for another two decades. By that time Electra I had died, and her share of the estate became the Wharton Estate. Guy died in 1950 and his share went to his surviving son, W. T. Waggoner, Jr. The Waggoner Estate bought W. T. Jr.'s share for an estimated $14 million in 1953, however he retained mineral rights. Paul was named executor of his mother Ella Halsell Waggoner's estate. He, having outlived his siblings, lived on the ranch and was active in the operation of the holdings until his death in 1967.

Mrs. Waggoner lived to be one hundred years old. In failing health for more than a year, she died May 17, 1959. At the time of her death Mrs. Waggoner lived at 1201 Hill Crest, near Fort Worth's Rivercrest Country Club. She willed $50,000 each to grandchildren W. T. Waggoner, Jr., A. B. Wharton, Jr., Ella Jean Waggoner Coberly, Elise Waggoner, and Electra II Waggoner Biggs. She gave the Hill Crest home to Electra II, and the rest of the estate went to her son, Paul. His son-in-law, John Biggs, managed the Vernon ranch.

The wills of W. T. and Ella Waggoner, though complex due

to the extensiveness of their wealth, were probated without dispute. Not so the wills of their children and grandchildren.

Electra I's trust fund left her one-third of the Waggoner Estate to be divided evenly between her two sons, Tom Waggoner Wharton and A. B. (Buster) Wharton, Jr. Tom W. Wharton died three years after his mother's death. He had no children, and his share of the trust went to his brother, A. B. Wharton, Jr.

Buster Wharton and his third wife, LaRita Thompson, had a son, A. B. (Bucky) Wharton III. Later Buster married Lula Link and adopted her daughter Reta Lorena (Link) Wharton. He was married to Lula at the time of his death in 1963 and she, Reta, and son Bucky, were the beneficiaries of his will.

The following year attorneys for the Waggoner Estate, the plaintiff, filed suit in Vernon's Forty-sixth District Court to overturn Buster's will. The legal question centered on whether he had the authority to will a trust established by his mother, Electra I, to his widow and adopted daughter. On April 9, 1964, papers filed to oust Lula Wharton from the sixteen-room house known as the Zacaweista residence stated:

"Since the acquisition of the Zacaweista residence by plaintiff in 1923, plaintiff has expended in excess of $200,000.00 (exclusive of maintenance costs) in adding to and remodeling said residence and in constructing and remodeling certain appurtenances and improvements adjacent to and surrounding said residence, including a swimming pool and bathhouse, a barbecue house, a greenhouse, a two-story native stone and frame guest house and garage, and two one-story servants quarters, all of which were constructed by plaintiff on its land and at its cost."[5]

The document listed employees, including A. B. Wharton, Jr., and residents of the house. Then continued,

"Defendant, Lula Judd Wharton, took up residence in the Zacaweista residence at or about the time of her marriage to A. B. Wharton, Jr., in June, 1949. Following the death of A. B. Wharton, Jr., on May 28, 1963, plaintiff's trustee concluded that it would be appropriate and proper to allow defendant, as the surviving wife of its deceased employee, to continue to occupy the Zacaweista residence temporarily, as an accommodation to her and at the will and by the sufferance of plaintiff, in order to give defendant a reasonable opportunity to find other and more permanent accommodations suitable to her station in life."[6]

She had no intention of leaving. "Defendant, however, through her attorney, has informed plaintiff that she will ignore the demands of plaintiff and will refuse to vacate the said improvements belonging to plaintiff. . . . contrary to law and in violation of plaintiff's right to possession."[7]

Things began to get nasty. "(a) Defendant, without authority, has removed locks from certain buildings and improvement of plaintiff and has replaced same with locks to which plaintiff has no keys, thereby preventing plaintiff from gaining access to such buildings. . . . which is necessary to plaintiff's business."[8]

Then things got worse. Lawyers for A. B. (Bucky) Wharton III argued that Lula Wharton's daughter, Reta, should not inherit from Electra I's trust.

Lula sued Killen M. Moore, a trustee of the Waggoner Estate. Married again, the suit lists her as Lula Wharton Van Hoose, executrix of the estate of Albert Buckman Wharton, Jr., deceased, et. al. Her lawyers included Elton M. Hyder, Jr., Thomas H. Law, Robert M. Randolph, and the firm of Stone, Tilley, Parker, Snakard, Law & Brown, all of Fort Worth.

Attorneys for Reta Lorena Wharton and the City National Bank in Wichita Falls, guardian of the estate of Reta Lorena Wharton, were Warren W. Shipman III, Kent D. Kibbie, the Fort Worth firm of McGown, Godfrey, Decker, McMackin, Shipman & McClane.

LaRita Rohla, Bucky's mother and guardian of the estate of Albert Buckman Wharton III, a minor, hired Fort Worth attorneys Edwin T. Phillips, Jr., his brother J. Olcott Phillips, Atwood McDonald, and George F. Christie of the firm of McDonald, Sanders, Wynn, Ginsburg, Phillips & Maddox. Joe Day, Jr., of Kerr, Day & Gandy also represented the interests of Bucky.

Thousands of pages of documents attest to the complexity of the case and matters leading up to it. For example, Edwin T. Phillips, Jr. stated "There is no genuine issue as to any material fact concerning who is the 'lawful issue' of Albert Buckman Wharton, Jr., as that term is used in the duly probated Last Will and Testament of Electra Waggoner, Deceased, dated March 19,

1925, and the Codicil thereto dated June 1, 1925. Albert Buckman Wharton, III, is the only natural born child of Albert Buckman Wharton, Jr., as that term is used in said Will and Codicil."[9]

A letter written October 26, 1954, from A. B. "Buster" Wharton, Jr. to his ex-wife LaRita concerning their son is part of the record. "As you know, Bucky will receive the income from this estate [The Electra I Waggoner Estate] at my death, and I thought you would like to know about this before any proceedings are started to change the trustee."[10] This was written shortly after the time that Ella Halsell Waggoner asked to be relieved of trustee duties and nine years before Buster's death.

Another letter introduced was written by him to his father, A. B. Wharton, Sr. Dated March 20,1959, it read:

"I don't think you fully understand all the complicated clauses in Mother's will, for if you did, you would know anything I might put in my will would be entirely up to the discretion of Bucky and the court."[11]

One of the clauses in Electra I's will dealt with "blood relatives." J. H. Barwise, Jr., senior member of the firm of Thompson and Barwise, wrote, "it was her purpose ... to will her property to her two children and for their use and benefit, and in event of the decease of her children without issue, then to her blood relatives, said will constituting a just and natural distribution of her property."[12]

The original petition of the Waggoner Estate, cited as Cause No. 88099 in the District Court of Wilbarger County, states "[held] in trust for A. B. Wharton, Jr., during the term of his natural life, and, upon his death, to deliver the same to his lawful issue, if any survive."[13]

The key phrase here was "lawful issue." Judge Thomas Davis ruled that Tom Wharton died without "lawful issue," and his share of the trust should go to his brother's estate. He cited the Texas Supreme Court decision of *Cutrer v. Cutrer* as the authority in this question. That case dealt with rights between an adoptive parent and an adopted child—the same relationship as Buster Wharton had with Reta. Despite the fact that Reta had been adopted at age three, and Wharton was the only father she had ever known, the crux of the matter was Electra I's will.

"The Texas Supreme Court held under trust instruments of third parties (in our case, Electra Waggoner) in which there was a distribution of corpus to adopting parent's (in our case Buster) children or heirs of the body, adopted child (in our case Rita [sic] Lorena Wharton) was not entitled to share," Judge Davis wrote.[14] He further noted that to find for Reta it would be necessary to determine that Electra I intended for "lawful issue" to include adopted children. "I can not find such an affirmative intention on the part of the Testarix in her will and codecil."[15]

Judge Davis in a ten-page "court's notification to counsel as to who is entitled to the assets of the Electra Waggoner Trust Estate" stated, "This court is of the opinion that Albert Buckman (Buster) Wharton Jr.'s only 'lawful issue,' as that term is used in the will and codecil of Electra Waggoner ... is Albert Buckman Wharton III, and as such is entitled to the corpus and accumulated income of the Electra Waggoner Trust Estate."[16]

Other claims were part of the suit, each grandchild and great-grandchild wanting their share of the estate. Guy L. Waggoner's granddaughters Jean Waggoner Coberly McCaughey, on behalf of her children William C. Coberly and Gary P. Coberly, sued for her grandfather's interest in the trust. She was represented by Charles L. Stephens of Cantey, Hanger, Gooch, Cravens & Scarborough. Ella Criss Waggoner Hay sued on behalf of her children Edward Lee Hay, Jr., Lynn Diane Hay, and Leslie Hay.

Appellants John Biggs and Electra II Waggoner Biggs, independent co-executors of the estate of E. Paul Waggoner, deceased, were represented by R. E. Hardwicke, Jr., Alex Pope, Jr., Larry K. Montgamer, and Beale Dean. Attorney General Crawford C. Martin, representing the interest of the University of Texas, was also a party to the suit.

The matter didn't end with Judge Davis's ruling. A suit was filed against A. B. "Bucky" Wharton, III on March 13, 1991. "The petition sought appointment of a receiver to liquidate and to distribute the W. T. Waggoner Trust Estate. In April of 1992, the court placed this case on the dismissal docket, but subsequently granted Plaintiff's Motion to Retain, allowing the case to remain on the docket. . . . As a result of the Plaintiffs' continued failure to prosecute this case with due diligence, the case was again placed on the Court's dismissal docket by letter dated January 18, 1996."[17]

Attorney E. Glen Johnson cited reasons for dismissal and requested the court "to refuse to consider an untimely Motion to Retain and seeks an order dismissing this case."[18]

It was not granted. As of March 31, 1999, the case was still pending.

Abridged Waggoner Family Tree in Narrative Form

From 1852 until the 1967 ruling of the 46th District Court

William Thomas Waggoner (8/1/1852-12/11/1934), married Ella Halsell (3/27/1859-5/17/1959).

Their children were: Dan E. Waggoner (1879-1881); Electra Waggoner (1/15/1882-11/26/1925); Willie Tom Waggoner (1885-1887); Guy Leslie Waggoner (9/21/1883-12/11/1950); and E. Paul Waggoner (4/9/1889-3/3/1967).

Electra married A. B. Wharton, Sr. Their children were Tom Waggoner Wharton (10/3/03-10/8/28) and A. B. (Buster) Wharton, Jr. (8/8/09-5/28/63). Electra also married Weldon M. Bailey and James A. Gilmore; no children from these two marriages.

Tom Waggoner Wharton married eight times, but had no heirs.

A. B. (Buster) Wharton, Jr. married four times. Wife LaRita Thompson Wharton (Rohla) was the mother of A. B. (Bucky) Wharton, III (10/1/47). Wife Lula Link Wharton (Van Hoose) was the mother of Lorena Link (11/15/47), whom A. B. Wharton, Jr. adopted in 1959.

Guy Leslie Waggoner married eight times, twice to Katherine Brown. They were the parents of W. T. Waggoner, Jr. (4/5/05-4/16/62). Guy Leslie Waggoner married Lucille Elliott. They were the parents of Guy L. Waggoner, Jr. (6/25/08-3/24/27).

W. T. Waggoner, Jr. and Elise Criss were the parents of Jean Waggoner McCaughey (4/25/62) and Elise Criss Waggoner Hay (7/2/33).

Jean married C. J. Coberly and had two children, William C. (7/8/58) and Gary P. Coberly (10/24/61).

Elise married Edward Lee Hay. They were the parents of Edward, Jr. (6/26/61), Lynn Dianne (1/19/63), and Leslie (2/22/64).

W. T. Waggoner, Jr. also married Mary Wilson and they were the parents of Jacqueline Waggoner (8/3/48).

Guy L. Waggoner, Jr. married Dorothy Scott. They had no children.

E. Paul Waggoner married Helen Buck. They were the parents of Electra Waggoner Biggs (11/8/12).

Electra married John Biggs. They were the parents of Electra Biggs (7/6/44) and Helen Biggs (4/30/46).

PART FOUR
The Lawyers

The Trailblazers

The glory days of Hell's Half Acre waned as the twentieth century rolled around. "Between 1900 and World War I, the Acre still had enough life left in it to raise an occasional tempest."[1] The murder of County Attorney Jefferson Davis McLean and the subsequent shootout between Sheriff Wood's deputies, local policemen, and assailant William (Bill) Tomlinson proved a perfect example.

In the words of the March 23, 1907, *Fort Worth Record and Register* front page account, this is what happened:

> Jefferson Davis McLean, shot through the neck which was broken and which resulted in instant death. . . .
> Hamill P. Scott . . . also shot in the axila of the right shoulder and in the right forearm. Death is expected momentarily. . . .
> William Tomlinson, shot through the stomach, in the right leg and in the fleshy part of the right shoulder. Rational when taken to city jail but later lost consciousness, and is expected to die at any moment.[2]

McLean was born and raised in Mount Pleasant, Texas, and even served as mayor before he came to Fort Worth in 1895. In Fort Worth he practiced law and was deputy county attorney under James Swayne. (County attorney later became the office of district attorney.) Elected county attorney in 1904, he was in his second term at the time of his death.

The bloodshed resulted from the raiding of the Stag Saloon, a gambling house owned by Tomlinson. The *Record and Register* reported that shortly after three o'clock the previous day, Sheriff Wood and several of his deputies arrested the card players and took them to the county jail.

County Attorney McLean and his wife were riding down Main Street when he noticed the sheriff returning to the saloon to remove the gambling paraphernalia. McLean, an ardent foe of open gambling, halted his buggy. Telling Mrs. McLean to wait for him, he approached Wood and offered to help. After the equipment was confiscated, McLean headed back to the buggy. He had gone but a few feet when he overheard Tomlinson grumbling about his gambling house being raided.

In the journalistic custom of that time, the *Record and Register* reported Tomlinson as saying, "There goes the – – – who always gets in when he ain't got a chance to get a piece of the pie for himself."[3] Not knowing what the – – – was, one must assume it was not flattering. As McLean walked toward Tomlinson, the gambler drew a .45 caliber pistol from his left hip pocket and fired.

County commissioner Duff Purvis witnessed the shooting. "I saw Jeff fall. I realized instantly what had taken place. I cried out to the crowd, 'Bill Thompson [*sic*] has shot Jeff; catch Bill.' I then turned to McLean. I wish I could describe the look on his face.... He looked like a man who had done his whole duty unflinchingly and he was not ashamed of what he had done."[4]

Tomlinson was accosted by Deputy Hamill P. Scott in an alley leading onto Seventh Street. Both men drew weapons and fired. Scott, hit in the neck, fell to the ground. Tomlinson, thinking the man dead, calmly took the deputy's pistol, then ran to Roe's Lumber Yard.

An angry crowd, estimated to be about 1,000 men and boys in the first part of the newspaper account, grew to 3,000 a few paragraphs later. Patrolman Dennis Loyd discovered the wanted man between two stacks of lumber. Both fired. Tomlinson was hit in the leg and shoulder. "At the sting of the second wound [Tomlinson] jumped from his crouching position and ran out into the opening where he encountered Policeman Bell, who immediately opened fire. The two men stood not over fifteen feet apart and in all exchanged eight shots, the last of which was fired from Bell's gun almost simultaneously with a charge from the gun of Policeman Loyd."[5] The crowd, estimated at over 4,000 men, women, and children by the last paragraph of the news account, watched as lawmen carted Tomlinson off to jail.

The gambler, fearing a lynch mob, feigned death. In the comparative safety of the jail hospital unit, he opened his eyes and talked to the attending physician. He confessed to bad blood between him and the county attorney and asserted the shooting was bound to happen sometime. In addition to the leg and shoulder wounds, Tomlinson sustained a fatal injury as one bullet entered the stomach and lodged too near the spine to be removed. He died at 7:30 the next evening.

Fort Worth officials had tried for years to remove the stigma of Hell's Half Acre and its accompanying reputation of a wide open town. This shooting, which occurred when hundreds of visitors were in town for the Cattlemen's Convention and Fat Stock Show, infuriated the citizenry. A mass meeting at the city hall was called for by, among others, B. B. Paddock. Leaders of the community declared the time was ripe to rid the city of gamblers and other lawbreakers. Shocked members of the Texas Legislature, in town for the stock show, upon their return to Austin passed a state law against gambling. Even a cursory examination of subsequent events reveals the lack of success of the well-intentioned measure.

The death of McLean seemed to bring to a close the era of wild west style shootouts between armed lawyers and armed civilians. He was accorded an elaborate funeral, with all the town dignitaries in attendance. Today a stained glass window in Hemphill Presbyterian Church is a reminder of the fallen county attorney.

In less flamboyant contributions, William Capps and Samuel Benton Cantey, Sr. also made headlines. Partners in the oldest continuously operating law firm in Fort Worth, they predated Jefferson McLean's term of office by thirty years. In 1881 the two opened a law office on the second floor of a building at Seventh and Main streets. "Both had been in practice before the formation of the partnership and their partnership, according to records and opinions, was a good combination. Mr. Cantey was a student of the law and Mr. Capps was innovative and it was said, practiced by intuition. Both were top flight trial lawyers," unofficial firm historian J. A. "Tiny" Gooch wrote.[6]

In 1999 the firm that bears the Cantey & Hanger name occupies two floors of the Burnett Plaza Building. Today's offices blend just the right mix of dark polished wood and glass with traditional furnishings and the latest in electronic equipment appropriate for such a firm.

Both Cantey and Capps were respected by the townspeople, but it was Capps that the Texas Rangers looked to for help in a volatile situation involving T. I. "Long Hair" Jim Courtright. Jim was a popular gambler-turned-Fort Worth marshal in the late 1870s. About the turn of the decade, he moved to New Mexico where he allegedly killed two ranchers. Fleeing that state, he returned to Fort Worth and operated a detective agency. In 1882 Courtright was arrested by Texas Rangers for the New Mexico crime.

An in-house history of the Cantey & Hanger law firm, titled *100 Years*, recounted, "Because of his rapport with his fellow citizens, the Rangers asked Capps to help calm the crowd, irate over the arrest of the popular Courtright. Capps mounted a shed over the window of the railroad ticket office . . . and reassured the crowd that Courtright would not be harmed."[7] While their attention was thus diverted the Rangers peacefully shuttled Courtright to the city jail.

Most of their work involved civil procedures. Toward the end of the nineteenth century, as unofficial lobbyists for the city, Cantey and Capps convinced Armour and Swift corporate directors to open meat packing houses in Fort Worth. They helped form the Stockyards Company, which acted as a gathering and sales place for supplying livestock to the packers. For decades that industry provided employment for thousands of North Texans. Today the romanticized stockyards area is a vital part of the city's tourist industry.

William M. Short joined in 1900. A graduate of Fort Worth University School of Law, he was admitted to the bar in 1899. His specialty was damage suits, but he was persuaded to defend

William Capps, original partner in Canty, Hanger LL.P.
—Photo courtesy Fort Worth Public Library Genealogy and Local History Department

a streetcar conductor on a charge of carrying a pistol aboard the car. Almost one hundred years later, a graduate of Texas Wesleyan University School of Law would say that the duty of a lawyer was to look at a set of facts differently. That's exactly what Short did. The fact was the conductor carried a weapon aboard the streetcar. Short did not deny it, but he argued his client had a right to possess a weapon at his place of business. And the conductor's place of business was the streetcar. Short won.

He was for many years a member and president of the Fort Worth School Board. As new partners came in, and others left, names were added or subtracted.

Cantey, a man of intellect and vision, continued to drive the firm forward. Realizing the importance of budding electric power, he brought to his firm the two largest holding companies in the nation—American Power & Light Company and Electric Bond & Share Company. In lieu of cash, Cantey accepted 100 shares of AP&L for his fee. "In the early 1900's Cantey traded his 100 shares of American Power and Light Company for a ranch stretching several thousand acres in Palo Pinto County."[8]

Later he persuaded the two companies to take a look at the market for electric generation and transmission in Fort Worth.

His efforts resulted in Fort Worth Power and Light, which ultimately became Texas Electric Service Company, now TXU.

Not resting on his laurels, Cantey and his firm next worked to bring mass transit to Fort Worth. The Stone and Webster Group of Boston worked with Cantey to form the Fort Worth Street Car Company, which later became the Fort Worth Transit Company.

"On the day of his funeral, in November, 1924, every streetcar in the city of Fort Worth stopped for three minutes in a unique and unprecedented tribute to Samuel Benton Cantey."[9]

Co-founder William Capps had died in 1919, but not before the firm had established itself as a powerhouse in Fort Worth's legal community.

W. A. Hanger, the next partner, served in the state senate, and was ever after referred to as "Senator." He joined the firm soon after the turn of the century. William was raised on a farm in what is now Forest Hill. He studied law at Cumberland University in Lebanon, Tennessee, and graduated in 1890. He returned to Texas but had to wait for his twenty-first birthday to begin his chosen profession. The Panic of 1893 was upon the country, and times were hard. "When I first started practicing law I didn't have enough to eat. And after 40 years I don't have time to eat," he recalled.[10]

Famous trial lawyer William A. Hanger was also a state senator.
—Photo courtesy Fort Worth Public Library Genealogy and Local History Department

Hanger found criminal law, with its drama and eloquent pleas to juries, the most attractive and lucrative area. His fame as a trial lawyer helped propel him into the senate in 1898. He served eight years and during that time he joined Capps and Cantey. The firm became known as Capps, Cantey, Hanger and Short.

The in-house historian noted, "Senator Hanger participated in several trials in which he served as counsel, including the investigations of Senator Joseph W. Bailey and James E. Ferguson."[11] (Bailey defended Frederick Cook; see page 116.) Ferguson was impeached as governor of Texas. Hanger remained active until his death in 1944. He was seventy-five years old and had been in practice for five decades.

When the firm outgrew its original quarters, it moved to the eleventh floor of the Burk Burnett Building. In 1930 Cantey, *et al.* moved to the newly constructed Sinclair Building at Fifth and Main. They occupied the fifteenth and sixteenth floors for the next thirty years.

Perry Cockerell, of the Cantey & Hanger firm, still exudes enthusiasm after seventeen years of practice when he speaks of the law. His interest was whetted at family reunions when his uncle, a prosecutor in Glen Rose, entertained young Perry with tales of the courtroom. The Texas Tech Law School graduate considers lawyers to be counselors as well as litigators. An important part of an attorney's responsibility to a client is to provide advice, counseling, and strategy on "how to shut down litigation."

When asked if he would advise a young person to enter the legal profession, he answered in the affirmative. "There's always a need for a lawyer because the law is related to everything we do."[12]

Another venerable firm that began in the last century was started when Morgan Bryan opened his office in the summer of 1892. It was in one room on the second floor of a building that later became Stripling's Department Store. Bryan formed a partnership with B. B. Stone, and the firm grew to what is now Law, Snakard & Gambill. Stone, a native of Ballinger, was active for fifty-seven years. During that time partners were added, some died, some left.

Caleb Pirtle, in an essay, wrote "By 1915 the firm was known as Bryan, Stone & Wade, and in that year it moved to the then Fort Worth National Bank Building at Fifth and Main Streets."[13] They counted the bank as one of their clients.

When Baylor Agerton returned from the military at the close of World War I, he joined the group. Under the name Bryan, Stone, Wade & Agerton, the firm prospered for the next thirty-three years.

Stone died in 1969 at the age of ninety-three, and the firm merged with Tilley, Hyder & Law, taking the name Law, Snakard, Brown & Gambill. Banking, corporate law, probate matters, oil and gas, real estate, and security regulations form the bulk of their practice. R. F. Snakard practiced law for forty-six years. He died in 1994 at age eighty-three.

A long list of civic accomplishments of firm members attest to their interest in the growth of Fort Worth and the well-being of its citizens. It has furnished two Fort Worth Chamber of Commerce presidents and a regent of the University of Texas system. Lawton L. Gambill was president of the Tarrant County Bar Association in 1937. Robert F. Snakard held that office in 1954. He was also the recipient of the Blackstone Award in 1978, as was Thomas H. Law in 1989. Lawyers in the firm have held numerous other civic and professional offices.

Now in its eleventh decade of continuous practice, Law, Snakard & Gambill is located at 500 Throckmorton.

Two years after Morgan Bryan started his practice, George Quentin McGown, another pioneer in the legal community, opened an office. The founder of the McGown law firm was born in 1860 in Charles County, Missouri, where he attended a "little red schoolhouse." His father, D. T. McGown, was for many years the Barton County, Missouri, judge.

McGown came to Fort Worth from Kansas in 1892 and operated a grocery store. During his first year in his adopted city he organized the Wholesale Credit Men's Association. He served as its secretary and manager for fifteen years.

McGown became interested in the law and studied at night for four years with Essex & Prigmore. W. S. Essex was attorney for Polytechnic College; one hundred years later McGown's great-grandson, George Quentin IV, would be a student at that institution's (now Texas Wesleyan University) law school. McGown (the elder, not the IV) was admitted to the bar on his birthday in 1896.

McGown's letterhead listed John C. Miller, George C. Ackers, H. T. McGown, S. H. Millwee, and A. C. Heath as members of the firm. It also listed clients "Clearing House Quarterly, C. R. C. Law List, Ass'n of Bonded Attorneys, Wilber Merc. Agency, Martindale's and Mercantile Adjuster."[14] In 1910 McGown sent the following announcement: "I am very much pleased to announce to my clients that Mr. Theodore A. Altman will occupy a desk in my office, commencing December first. Mr. Altman is late of Burnett, Texas, and formerly of the law firm of Flournoy & Altman, of this city."[15] He included in the announcement the areas of specialization for his staff. "Mr. T. A. Altman will be responsible for all business in the 17th, 48th, and 67th District Courts and the two County Courts of this City; Mr. John C. Miller will be responsible for all business originating in Courts outside of the City and including the United States District Court and Bankrupt Courts."[16] In like manner he listed the responsibilities of each member of the firm. This public notice would be impossible today with some firms having as many as seventy-five to a hundred lawyers on the staff.

As attorney for the Fort Worth Retail Grocers' Association, McGown specialized in collections for grocers and dry goods merchants. In that capacity

Winfield Scott Essex, attorney for Polytechnic College, was mentor for G. Q. McGown, 1892-1896.
—Photo courtesy Fort Worth Public Library Genealogy and Local History Department

he wrote to Anchor Roller Mills a letter dated December 31, 1909.

"In regard to your account against I. R. Darwood of Wortham, beg to advise you that this account was closed up by accepting a note for $263.50 and a Deed for a lot in Hamlin and ten acres of land as shown by the Deed. . . . I believe we will be able to make a sale of this property and if you desire and will return me the Deed and this letter I will follow it up with other correspondence and see if we can not dispose of it to an advantage. The cost, traveling expense, etc. is $5.90, recording the Deed $1.00, one day's service $10.00, total $16.90, which I am deducting from a remittance made you today in claim No. 11898, yours vs. W. T. Box at Runge."[17] It was signed Geo. Q. McGown.

In 1911, McGown formed a partnership with his eldest son, Harry T. McGown. The two practiced together until 1928. When George Q., Sr. retired, George Q., Jr. became a partner. The founder died in 1940, two years after the firm became known as McGown, McGown, Godfrey and Logan. By the time of George Q. McGown, Sr.'s death the firm had become one of the most respected in the city.

Harry McGown was born in Wellington, Kansas, but grew up in Fort Worth. After attending public schools here, he graduated from the University of Texas. McGown was a member of the Fort Worth Boat Club, Phi Delta Phi, and several other professional and social organizations. He had been in ill health for a number of years and died at the age of fifty-six.

George McGowen, grocer-turned-lawyer, founded his firm in 1896.
—Photo courtesy of the McGown family

Harry T. McGown practiced law with his father and brother.

—Photo courtesy of the McGown family

Attorney George Q. McGown, Jr. was born in Fort Worth. He was a graduate of Columbia University and received his LL.B. from Cumberland University in 1924. Like his older brother, Harry, he was an avid yachtsman. He served as commodore of the Snipe Class International Sailing Association and was a charter member and first commodore of the Fort Worth Boat Club. George McGown, Jr. attained the rank of lieutenant commander in the Navy during World War II and organized the first Naval Reserve Unit in the city.

The McGown firm specialized in corporate law and counted businesses such as furniture manufacturer A. Brandt and Company and Haltom's Jewelers as clients. George Jr. was a member of the American Bar Association, the State Bar of Texas, and the Fort Worth-Tarrant County Bar Association. At one time he was chairman of the board of Howell Instruments, Inc.

Mr. McGown was an honorary member of the Fort Worth Legal Secretaries Association. Perhaps long-time secretary Margaret Fenlon had something to do with that. Quentin IV remembered Miss Margaret as a driving force in his grandfather's office, and his childhood Saturday and school holiday visits were to see her as much as to see his grandfather.

At the time of his death in 1977, George Q., Jr. was retired as senior partner of McGown, Godfrey, Decker, McMackin, Shipman & McClane.

George Quentin McGown III loved sailing as much as his

father did. It was only natural that he should serve
in the U.S. Navy. From
1957 to 1960 he was the
Naval Postmaster in
Yokohama, Japan. The
University of Texas Law
School graduate chose
general practice upon his
return to Fort Worth. His
son, Quentin IV, plans to
continue the family tradition upon his graduation
from Texas Wesleyan
University School of Law.

*George Q. McGown III followed
in his father's footsteps.*
—Photo courtesy of the
McGown family

*Historian G. Quentin McGown IV will be
a fourth generation Fort Worth attorney.*
—Photo courtesy of the McGown family

Legendary Lawyers

An individual hailed as having one of the great legal minds of the first half of the century was Sidney L. Samuels. He served as city attorney from 1907 to 1909. A self-described "unreconstructed Southerner," critics could fault him for his devotion to a lost cause, but none would deny his eloquence in the courtroom or on a dais. His father was a captain in the Confederate Army; his mother from genteel Mississippi stock. He inherited from them a sense of honor, integrity, and regard for the "aristocracy of intelligence."

Samuels attended the old Fort Worth University. When he decided to go to the University of Texas, his mother offered her jewelry as security for a loan to pay his tuition. *Star-Telegram* reporter Mabel Gouldy noted: "He did three years work in one year and as a result had to wait until he was 21 to start his practice."[1] A frail young man, he almost wrecked his health in his efforts to get the law degree.

His legal specialization was libel law, representing many magazines of national circulation as well as the *Fort Worth Star-Telegram*. As attorney for the latter, he once defended the newspaper when a Southern Methodist University cheerleader sued the newspaper after a reporter used the word "hussy" to describe the Texas Christian University opponent.

In a more serious vein, Samuels and J. C. Muse, attorney for the *Dallas Morning News*, wrote the "Texas privilege statute which enables newspapers to publish sworn courtroom testimony."[2]

Samuels was known nationally as a strict constitutionalist. In 1939 he sat on the bench of the Texas Supreme Court as a special chief justice. The case involved 28,000 acres of Panhandle public grazing lands that rancher Gus Wortham wanted to buy. A historian of note, Samuels turned down Wortham's plea, citing Texas tradition. Toward the end of his ruling, Samuels wrote, "A statute should not be construed in a spirit of detachment as if it were protoplasm floating in space. A literal interpretation of the statute which denies to it the historical circumstances under which it is drawn is to make mummery of its provisions."[3]

A lover and collector of rare books, he nevertheless fought the building of a new library. When the city planned to build it in Burk Burnett Park, Samuels objected on the grounds its location violated the terms of the will he had written for Burnett. The library was built on Throckmorton Street instead.

In addition to print media, his clients included the Tarrant County Water Control Board, and he was personal attorney to Amon Carter Sr. and Capt. S. Burk Burnett.

Samuels's civic activities span five decades. He served on the appeals section of the draft board in World War I, and was a community leader in the 1930s and 1940s. In 1953 Governor Allan Shivers appointed him to the Historical Society Committee. That eighteen-member group was charged with investigating the possibility of establishing a historical foundation. By their work thousands of landmarks and documents have been saved for future generations.

Samuels was politically conservative. Throughout his life he supported states' rights and viewed mid-century efforts of civil rights activists as unconstitutional. Speaking to the San Antonio Rotary Club in the summer of 1948 he declared, "An excess of liberty is anarchy, and men recoil at it. . . . An excess of law is tyranny, at which we are revolted. . . . Our great task is to combine liberty and law to the best of our ability, in the spirit of our ancestors who strived for a balanced government."[4] He opposed what he saw as the "infection of socialism" brought on by Franklin D. Roosevelt's New Deal. "What we need, . . . is a leisure class, a class unprivileged but with the aristocracy of intelligence, pledged to service of the people and the state, something comparable to the gentry of the Old South," he told the Rotarians.[5]

Samuels supported Dwight D. Eisenhower for the presidency, but became disenchanted with the World War II hero over social issues in the 1950s. He told the Kiwanis Club of North Fort Worth, "When Eisenhower visited the South and Southern governors risked their political lives by supporting him, you'd think he at least would not have encouraged his attorney general to appear before the Supreme Court and advocate abolition of segregation."[6]

As a speaker he had few equals. Samuels was chosen in 1940 to represent the State Bar of Texas for the keynote address of the special session marking the centennial of the State Supreme Court's location in Austin. In his speech entitled "Love of Liberty," he proclaimed to that august body, "Our children throughout the land should be told in the classroom how civil liberty has been cradled and cherished through the courts, and how the gospel of individual freedom has been the theme of holy texts in hundreds of decisions that guard the people from harm and protect them even as against themselves."[7]

In late 1957 friends and city leaders met to honor him with speeches of their own. Two hundred-fifty laymen and lawyers attended the testimonial dinner at the Hotel Texas' Crystal Ballroom. Judge Tom Renfro, formerly with Samuels's law firm, lauded him as the most remarkable man he had ever known. "I wish I could pay tribute to Sidney Samuels with some of the eloquence of Sidney Samuels," he told the assembled guests.[8] He went on to say that not only were lawyers who worked with Samuels better lawyers, but all who associated with him were better men for it.

Harold Hough, a *Star-Telegram* vice president, apologized "for only being able to use five and six syllable words" in the presence of the oratorical and scholarly honoree.

Samuels had his lighter side, according to long-time associate W. L. Pier, vice president of Tarrant County Savings & Loan, where Samuels had been a director since its beginning in 1921. He summarized his colleague's legal guideline as believing it was more important to keep your clients out of trouble than to wait and then get them out of trouble.

Slightly less than a year after the lavish testimonial dinner, the governor, judges, and colleagues again spoke of the greatness of the lawyer; this time at his funeral. Samuels fell on the steps of his home in September 1958 and was confined to bed. He died November 29, 1958.

Governor Price Daniel sent condolences to the family, noting his death "was a great loss to the legal profession and to our state."[9] Leo Brewster, speaking as president of the State Bar of Texas said, "Mr. Samuels was regarded by all who knew him as one of the great lawyers in the history of Texas. His learning, modesty and gentility were an inspiration to those who came in contact with him."[10] Sidney L. Samuels willed his 7,000-volume library to Texas Wesleyan College.

Another lawyer described as a genteel man, a gentleman in every sense of the word, was Forrest Markward. His boyhood idol was his uncle, John Edward Hickman, who served on the Texas Supreme Court. Young Forrest tried to emulate him by going into law, and by becoming "a good person."

Markward is reticent to speak of his accomplishments, but colleagues are not so silent. They point out he served as president of the Tarrant County Bar Association, received an honorary doctorate from Texas Wesleyan University School of Law, and was given the acclaimed Blackstone Award, along with many other recognitions.

His career actually started in the oil fields. Shortly after passing the bar exam, Markward spent several months with an oil company surveying crew. He remembered the work as helpful in his law practice.

The Great Depression was coming to an end, but times were still bad when he joined the firm of Calloway, Wade & Davis. Markward was given office space, but had to generate his own clientele. To make ends meet, he moonlighted as a bookkeeper for $25.00 a month.

At the beginning of World War II, and after three years as a struggling lawyer, he was drafted and stationed at Camp Walters. "I was one of the few people inducted into the Army at an increase in pay," he said with a grin.[11] While stationed in the South Pacific, "the young U.S. Army officer received a key assignment—to write a document that the Japanese commanding general could sign at the surrender of Mindanao in the Philippines at war's end."[12]

Call it fate or being in the right place at the right time, another momentous event unexpectedly came his way. On that fateful November day in 1963, Markward was on his way to work when follow attorney Eldon Mahon offered him a ticket to the Hotel Texas breakfast where President John F. Kennedy was the speaker. "Later, Markward represented Marina Oswald, whose husband, Lee Harvey Oswald, was accused of killing Kennedy. Markward prepared a trust fund with donations sent to Marina Oswald, who was left a widow with two young children after Jack Ruby fatally shot her husband."[13]

With characteristic modesty he depicted the episode as just trying to help someone who needed it.

Markward concentrated on general civil law, oil and gas work, and some estate planning. In all of these he saw beyond the briefs and legal language to the people. "Woven together they make a story," he said.[14]

Markward retired in 1999 after sixty years of practice. When asked the biggest changes over those years, he thought for a moment, then replied "technology." As he sorted through boxes and stacks of documents in preparation of closing his office, he came across a handwritten abstract dated in 1910. He fondly reminisced about the old days when a pen was a lawyer's most important tool. He accepted the use of the typewriter to replace handwritten documents, but he leaves the computer technology to others.

Among the memorabilia given to the Tarrant County Bar Association is a copy of the May 1948 *Fort Worth Bar News* addressed to Forrest Markward, Jr., W. T. Waggoner Bldg.; Fort Worth 2, Texas. On it is a canceled one cent stamp. The newsletter list of officers includes: "Oliver W. Fannin, President; Harry K. Brown, Past President; R. V. Nichols, Vice-President; Luther Hudson, Vice-President; and Olcott Phillips, Secy-Treas."[15]

A professional and a traditionalist, it is only fitting that the courthouse flagpole bears this inscription: "To Forrest Markward: A gentleman of the old school."

Winfred Hooper, 1999 Blackstone Award co-receipent, like Markward, remembers the Great Depression. He grew up in the small West Texas town of Wink. At age thirteen he was working odd jobs to augment the family income. In 1941, he recalled, "Most of the men went off to war and left the children and old men to carry on the work in the oil field. While in high school Win worked . . . on rotary drilling rigs."[16]

He attended Texas Tech for one year as a chemical engineering major, then joined the Marines on his eighteenth birthday. According to the *Tarrant County Bar Association Bulletin*, "Just as he was finishing bootcamp in San Diego, . . . the war was over, so he didn't have to go fight."[17] He was trained as a Morse Code radio man, could type eighty-five w.p.m., but it was his experience as a witness in a court-martial that set him on the road to law school. Fascinated with the legal proceedings, he returned to Tech and switched from chemical engineering to government. He graduated with a B.A. in 1950.

Hooper spent another year in the oil field, this time saving money for law school. "He graduated in the top quarter of his class and was Phi Delta Phi from the University of Texas, with his J.D. in 1954," the *Bulletin* noted in its profile of Hooper.[18]

He received offers from several cities, but chose to begin his career with the Fort Worth firm of McGown, Godfrey, Logan & Decker as a trial lawyer. "Win says his mentoring came from opposing attorneys, beginning with his first trial six weeks out of law school against Ardell Young, who was the most exceptional trial lawyer around at the time and who soundly defeated him."[19]

Learning from his mistakes, the 1957 personal injury case against the City of Fort Worth and Casino Beach Amusement Park made history. His client, paralyzed from a diving injury, was awarded $248,000. That was an unprecedented sum in those days.

In another case he showed his courtroom savvy in the presentation of physical evidence. His client, Pangburn Candy Company, was famous for its holiday chocolates. The company made candy year-round and kept it in cold storage until Valentine's Day, Mother's Day, or whatever special occasion called for it to be marketed. They purchased a double-stick tape from the Minnesota Mining & Manufacturing Company to seal the packages of candy. To their horror, Pangburn discovered that a chemical odor from the tape contaminated some 150,000 boxes of candy, their entire production. Hooper sued 3M for damages. There was a big stink at the trial. "Hooper showed his witness, a Pangburn representative, an unopened package of the tape. The witness identified it as tape bought from 3M, and verified it was in its original wrapping. He (Hooper) broke the wrapping and set the tape on the court reporter's desk."[20] Within minutes the odor was so strong the judge was forced to call a recess until the courtroom could be ventilated. Hooper's client, one might say, came out smelling like a rose.

The *Star-Telegram* story announcing the Blackstone Award stated, "Hooper went on to represent such clients as relatives of test pilots killed in helicopter crashes, and Dallas billionaire Harold Simmons in a fraud suit filed by the state."[21]

In his long career Winfred Hooper was prominent in professional and civic activities according to the bar journal. "He has served as President of the Fort Worth-Tarrant County Trial Lawyers Association, as Advocate of the American Board of Legal Specialization for the State Bar of Texas, and as President of the Eldon B. Mahon Inn of Court."[22] For these and many other contributions to the legal community the Tarrant County Bar Association recognized Hooper with its 1999 Blackstone Award. Not resting on his laurels, the oil field roustabout turned lawyer says he plans to keep practicing until he's ninety years old.

One of Hooper's colleagues is Kleber Miller. A most respected trial lawyer, he too is active in professional activities. He served as 1967 president of the Tarrant County Bar Association, and in 1991 was honored by that group with the coveted Blackstone Award. In discussing the practice of law today, he was asked about what appears to be an exploding growth of litigation. "Yes, it seems so, but the numbers don't support it," he said.[23] He conceded that people do file law suits more now without trying to work things out. "Mediation frequently comes after law suits are filed, rather than before."

Miller is optimistic about the future of the law. For young people looking for a profession, he told an interviewer, "if they like people, like solving disputes and can work under pressure, they can derive a lot of satisfaction from practicing law."[24]

Judge L. Clifford Davis also sees a bright future for young people, especially in the emerging fields of communication and environmental law. Davis, a 1949 graduate of Howard University

School of Law, was a major player in the civil rights movement of the 1950s and 1960s. His lawsuit against the Fort Worth Board of Education, *Flax v. Potts*, resulted in the integration of the school district.

That litigation was perhaps the most far-reaching, but the retired judge, in a recent interview, recalled a case that was equally important to him. "There was a lady who lived in the Butler Housing Projects on $93.00 a month from Social Security. Some kids playing nearby broke a window in her apartment," he said. The project rules

Judge L. Clifford Davis, pioneer in the Civil Rights Movement, led the fight for school desegregation.
—Photo Courtesy of Judge Davis

required tenants to replace broken windows, in her case, at the cost of $8.00. "That was a lot of money to her." He got a waiver as part of his mission to "make life better for people."[25]

In addition to his civil rights work, Davis negotiated behind the scenes to improve housing for minorities. For these and other contributions to the community, he was honored with the Silver Gavel Award by the Tarrant County Bar Association in 1997. That same year Davis was inducted into the National Bar Association Hall of Fame.

Lawyers and Politics

Many lawyers find satisfaction in combining their law practice with politics. At any given session of the Texas Legislature, a large number of representatives and senators have a background in law.

Joe Shannon, Sr., at age eighteen, cut his political teeth campaigning for gubernatorial candidate Tom Hunter, but his interest in law predated that campaign. In high school he determined to combine a career in law and politics. Barely old enough to meet the constitutional age requirement, Shannon ran for state representative in 1935, finished first in a ten-man race, but lost in the runoff.

The North Texas School of Law graduate was admitted to the bar in 1938. He practiced with the Otis Rogers and Joe Spurlock, Sr. firm until World War II.

Shannon was in the Air Crops from 1942 until 1945 and served as a tailgunner on B-17s during thirty-two missions over Europe, earning the Air Medal with three Oak Leaf Clusters and the Distinguished Flying Cross.[1] After the war he was an assistant in District Attorney Al Clyde's office, where he worked with Eva Bloore Barnes.

In 1948 Shannon won election to the Texas House of Representatives by a 10,000 vote majority. It was a family affair, with wife Juanita, and "campaign manager" seven-year-old Joe Jr. helping out. Joe Jr. ". . . never missed a night political meeting or a chance to push cards. But even little Joe is glad that the campaign is over and won so that he can resume his usual schedule of ball games and Saturday afternoon movies," the *Star-Telegram* reported.[2] Shannon served two terms, and later practiced law with his son until his death in 1975. Joe Shannon, Jr. followed in his father's footsteps, first becoming a lawyer, then an assistant district attorney, and state representative.

Professor Joe Spurlock II comes from a political family.
—Photo courtesy TWU School of Law

Another father-son political combination was Joe Spurlock, Sr. and Joe II. But this family could be considered father-son-mother, because Mrs. Spurlock represented the Meadowbrook and East Fort Worth areas on the city council in the 1950s. "I've been in politics since I was four years old," the younger Spurlock said in an interview.[3] He started by handing out matches at political rallies, and putting flyers under people's car windshield wipers. As he got older he helped stuff envelopes, and once commented, "I still remember those paper cuts." As he grew up he performed almost every chore around a campaign office. The affable man with the bushy mustache recalled the days before air-conditioned halls and the thirty-second television sound bite. "We campaigned at night, it was cooler. We'd go to an open field and everyone would head-in, park in a circle and leave their headlights on. The candidates would make speeches by those lights."[4]

Spurlock truly came from a multigenerational political family. His grandfather was sheriff of Throckmorton County, his father was first judge of the Ninety-sixth District Court and subsequently went to the Second Court of Appeals. A rarity, both father and son were judges at the same time.

Joe Spurlock II graduated from the University of Texas School of Law and passed the bar in 1962. It was the period of the Vietnam War and he saw action there. After his military discharge he worked in 1967 in District Attorney Frank Coffey's office for three years.

He served in the state legislature for seven years. Perhaps the most user-friendly bill he voted for allowed for drivers to make a right turn after stopping at a red light, unless prohibited by signs. Motorists have him and his colleagues to thank for untold hours of time saved and millions of gallons of gasoline not wasted as a result of that simple law.

Spurlock supported two of his colleagues: Kay Bailey, now Hutchison, and Sarah Weddington, both members of the legislature. Although politically they were on opposite ends of the spectrum, they both lobbied with Spurlock for the 1973 Equal Rights Amendment. The amendment passed, and it did away with restrictions on married women to contract in their own right. Today when Professor Spurlock tells his young law students that at one time women were legally classified in the same category as minors, idiots, the insane, or criminals, "They are astonished to learn that it's been so recently that a woman had to have a husband, father, or judge to approve a simple contract for her."[5]

Following his years in the legislature, Spurlock was on Governor Dolph Briscoe's staff. Later he was the first judge of the 231st District Court, and succeeded his father on the Second Court of Appeals. Although now retired after twenty-three years on the bench, he takes occasional cases as a visiting judge.

Spurlock holds an LL.M. degree from the University of Virginia Law School. At Texas Wesleyan University School of Law as adjunct professor, he teaches a course on family law, contracts, and legislation. He also teaches at the University of Michigan, the University of Texas at Arlington, and Tarrant County College as adjunct professor. He has served as president of the Texas Judicial Council, and was voted Adjunct Professor of the Year for 1990-1991. The following year he was named by Delta Theta Phi International Law Fraternity as Outstanding Faculty Member in the Nation.

When asked if he would encourage one of his children to go into law, he said, "Absolutely!" He has a nine-year-old daughter who wants to be a judge. "Straight to the bench," he laughed.[6]

Don Gladden, another lawyer/politician, got into his vocation by accident, one might say. During World War II he dropped out of high school, lied about his age, and joined the Navy. He and a buddy were on leave in Long Beach, California. "Some bottles were sitting in the alley at the property line. I threw a whiskey bottle down an alley and hit a wall," he recalled.[7] What he didn't know was that a policeman was parked behind the wall and was sprinkled with shattered glass. "Gladden said he was persuaded to 'confess' after more than three hours of personal attention by Long Beach's finest and 'seven or eight slaps in the nose.'"[8]

He planned to go into medicine when he got out of the Navy, but after his arrest he came to believe there was a greater need for lawyers than doctors. Many years later he related his adventures in a friendly conversation with the chief of police of the City of Fort Worth. "If they'd done what they should have done to you, you'd have realized there was more need for doctors than lawyers." the chief chuckled.[9]

Gladden enrolled in what was then Texas Wesleyan College one

Don Gladden was honored in 1999 for contributions as "Lawyer of the Masses."
—Photo courtesy of
Don Gladden

semester before his high school class graduated. He earned a B.S. in 1951 and went to the University of Texas to study law. Licensed in 1954, he served four terms in the Texas House of Representatives, from 1959 to 1968.

He has been called "the lawyer for the masses" as a result of his efforts to repeal the poll tax, a not-too-subtle device aimed at preventing minorities and the poor from voting. The "lawyer for lost causes," as one newspaper reporter labeled him, has spent years in his untiring efforts to reverse what he sees as civil rights violations. Two successful endeavors stand out: non-property owners' voting rights, and single member districts.

In the 1960s Fort Worth had two ballot boxes, one for property owners, the other for non-property owners. Proponents of the system argued that only those who paid property taxes should determine how those taxes were spent. Gladden held non-property owners had a stake in city services by virtue of paying rent which indirectly went for property taxes.

The case at hand involved a bond issue on building a new library. Property owners voted the measure down, but non-property owners' votes would be enough to put it over the top. He carried the fight to the nation's highest court. As a result of his lawsuit, the library was built, and the Supreme Court declared separate ballots for the two classes of residents illegal. His victory went beyond the city limits. The court's ruling led to case law that allowed El Paso, with a similar situation, to issue bonds to build a junior college.

Gladden also led a battle for single member legislative districts. It took sixteen years of lawsuits and appeals before the Supreme Court upheld his contention that minorities did not have equal access under the "at large" system. The *News-Tribune* noted the price he paid for the victory was a great one, both in time and cash outlays.

Starting in 1961 Gladden fought to change the system whereby representatives were elected by voters from throughout the county. It was expensive for all candidates to campaign, thus favoring incumbents. Based on the 1960 census, he presented his single member district plan, hoping for it to be approved by the 1976 elections. The *News Tribune*, in recapping the legal fight, declared, "Actually, Gladden's plan was first adopted by a majority of the three-judge court in 1974, but an appeal to Supreme Court Justice Lewis Powell stayed that order and left Tarrant County under the old at-large system for one last time."[10]

The following year, 1975, the Legislature passed Rep. Bud Sherman's single member district plan, but the Justice Department vetoed it under the federal Voting Rights Act. In 1976 Fifth Circuit Court of Appeals Judge Irving Goldberg, and District Judges William W. Justice and John Wood adopted the plan put forward by Rep. Tom Schieffer. "But the court left the way open for Gladden to return to the courthouse after the 1976 elections, and he did," the *Tribune* noted.[11] This time the court ruled in favor of Gladden's plan, which put neighborhoods of common social and economic needs in a district. In 1978, for the first time in a century, Tarrant County had minority representatives. Gladden, an ardent Democrat, brought about another outcome. Under his plan a Republican was elected also.

For these and other civil rights cases, Gladden was honored by the Tarrant County Bar Association with its 1999 Blackstone Award.

To say that Gladden has been engaged in the general practice of law from 1954 until the present with "some emphasis on civil rights litigation" is to say people in Washington, D.C. are somewhat interested in politics. Sometimes for no fee, sometimes for a substantial court-ordered settlement, if Gladden thinks someone has been wronged, he'll take the case.

He is a member of the State Bar of Texas, the Tarrant County Bar Association, the Tarrant County Criminal Defense Lawyers Association, the American Civil Liberties Union, and the National Lawyers Guild. He is admitted to practice before the Texas Supreme Court, the U.S. Supreme Court, the Court of Appeals for the Fifth and Ninth Circuits of the U.S., and the U.S. District Courts for the Northern District and the Western District of Texas.

He is either angel or devil because of his civil rights work. The masses love him; the "establishment" loathes him.

Gladden has two sons who are practicing attorneys and his daughter, before her recent death, was his office manager. Will his sons follow dad's footsteps to Austin?

"We'll have to wait and see," he said as he thumbed through a scrapbook of his legislative and legal adventures.[12]

The Tarrant County Bar Association

"**I**f we are to consider ourselves public servants then we must serve the public, and to sit on the porch and rock in silence is not the best way to serve the public."[1] The Tarrant County Bar Association has certainly taken jurist Charles Murray's words to heart. In 1998 the Tarrant County Bar Association celebrated seventy years of service to the community.

It was a celebration well-deserved. George M. Conner was the TCBA's first president. Since his tenure in office a veritable "Who's Who" within the legal community has led the organization. Beale Dean, 1971 president, and Judge Steve King are working on archival projects to preserve the history of the association. The TCBA also sponsored the reprinting of the memoirs of pioneer lawyer Captain J. C. Terrell as part of the 1999 Fort Worth Sesquicentennial Celebration.

Among those archives one finds evidence of opportunities for professional growth, social interaction, and at times witness to advocacy. In 1937 Bar Association President Zeno C. Ross signed a resolution concerning President Franklin D. Roosevelt's attempt to expand the number of Supreme Court justices.

WHEREAS, under our system of representative democratic government . . . [citizens' rights to express opinions].

WHEREAS, since the Judicial branch of our Government must and does follow the worthy practice of remaining silent when its functions and acts are publicly assailed, it is deemed particularly proper that, with respect to legislation affecting the Judiciary, and views and opinions of all citizens be publicly and respectfully expressed; and

WHEREAS, the President's proposal to Congress that he be authorized to increase the membership of the Supreme Court of the United States to fifteen members, if members thereof over seventy years of age do not voluntarily retire, is considered by the Fort Worth Bar Association to be untimely, unsound and objectionable for numerous reasons, including these: . . .[2]

The document stated five objections suggesting infringement upon the separation of powers, negating the checks and balances provided for in the Constitution and endangering the independence of the Court. History supported their resolution, and the legislation failed.

The Nominations Committee mails ballots for officers and directors in March. Members return their marked ballots, and the winners are installed. But the 1960 election was somewhat different. The office of president was decided by a coin toss. Attorneys Bob Maddox and Joe Edison received the same number of votes. "As prescribed in the by-laws, association directors summoned the two to the Civil Court Building and settled the issue by lot. First, a coin was flipped, and Maddox called the toss correctly. That gave him a first draw from a packet of pamphlets, one of which was marked 'president' inside. Maddox drew the right one."[3] Edison was elected to the post in 1966.

By tradition TCBA presidents and its executive committees have sought to enhance professional growth by providing members with opportunities to hear outstanding guest speakers. Attorney General Waggoner Carr, in early 1964, spoke on crime prevention and upcoming legislation. TCBA President Kleber C. Miller welcomed such notables as Ben Barnes, Speaker of the Texas House of Representatives, the Honorable Thomas M. Phillips, president of the State Bar of Texas, and the Honorable John L. Hill, secretary of state, when they addressed the group in 1967.

Former President Olcott Phillips, writing in *The Bar News*, forerunner of the *TCBA Bulletin*, wrote in February 1969 that the cost of monthly luncheons had increased from $2.55 to $2.80, but noted the quality of programs more than compensated for the increased cost.

That same issue detailed meeting dates for the Fort Worth Legal Secretaries Association annual seminar. The March 13 topic was "'The Professional Legal Secretary,' presented by E. L. 'Max' Hamilton, Assistant Executive Director of the State Bar Association."[4] Other programs were Judge Eva Barnes' presentation on "Domestic Relations Court," and "Civil Procedures and the Legal Secretary," by Winfred Hooper.

United States District Judge William M. Taylor was the guest speaker at a luncheon in October 1972. His topic was "Observations on Federal Practice." In 1972 Robert W. Calvert, chief justice of the Supreme Court of Texas, was honored at a dinner given by the Bar Association. U. S. Treasury Secretary John B. Connally, a former governor and former Fort Worth attorney, was the keynote speaker.

Throughout the decades of the seventies and eighties, similarly important programs were slated. One program was an indication of gender changes in the legal profession. The occasion was when the Fort Worth-Tarrant County Young Lawyers Association and the TCBA joined to present Assistant United States Attorney Terri Moore in October 1998. In the *Tarrant County Bar Association Bulletin* announcing her presentation, it was noted, "Ms. Moore received her B.A. from Texas Christian University in 1981 and her J.D. from South Texas College of Law in 1986."[5]

Membership in the Tarrant County Bar Association is open to all Tarrant County attorneys, including sitting judges, in good standing with the state bar. Associate memberships are open to others in the legal community such as paralegals and students.

Today, more than fifty committees work to promote the goals of the association. The usual bylaws, continuing legal education, membership, nominations and publications committees are joined by several unique ones. As the name implies, the Bench Bar Conference Committee plans an annual conference for Tarrant County attorneys; the Fee Arbitration Committee conducts hearings on fee disputes between lawyers and clients; and the Law Day Committee is responsible for the annual Law Day Luncheon, the Law Day Scholarship, and the Silver Gavel Award.

The Judicial Polls Committee, according to their guidelines, "develops and distributes in election years, a judicial candidate qualification and judicial preference poll, and in non-election years, a judicial evaluation poll. The Committee is responsible for disseminating the result of these polls to members of the public."[6]

To help lawyers meet the needs of domestic abuse victims, the Lawyers Against Domestic Violence Committee conducts seminars on the handling of these difficult cases.

Wade H. McMullen, 1998-1999 president, is especially enthusiastic about the committees "that give back to the community." He indicated there are about thirty set up to do that, based on two guidelines. One is an obligation to help people who can't afford legal representation at the regular fee rate. Bar members agree to provide thirty-minute consultations at a cost of only $20.00, which is only a fraction of what it normally would cost. Those unable to pay even the minimal charge are given free services. Volunteers have found that sitting down with someone who may think he or she has a huge problem, but in thirty minutes can be advised of the seriousness, or lack thereof, and how to handle the problem, has been a tremendous help to the public.

McMullen told of an elderly woman who was terrified that a letter she had received a month before his visit to her senior citizen center meant she was about to be sued. He read the letter and explained it was merely a tax evaluation. Moreover, he told her how to get a senior exemption. In those brief moments, he relieved her of an enormous burden. "Every lawyer holds the key to legal knowledge because we're trained that way. . . . and because we hold that key, our Board thinks we have a special obligation to give back to the community," he is fond of saying.[7] More than 200 lawyers participate in this program.

The other way lawyers help is through the Legal Line project of the bar association. Lawyers answer legal questions over the phone the second and fourth Thursdays of each month between 6:00 and 8:00 P.M. They can also refer clients to agencies or places already set up to help them. Thus clients are steered in the direction they need to go and "if the lawyers didn't agree to help them, who knows how long it would take them to get something resolved, or how much it would cost them to get something resolved that really shouldn't cost them that much," McMullen declared.[8]

The *Star-Telegram* named the Tarrant County Bar Association as the winner of its prestigious 1998 "Club of the Year"

President Wade McMullen addressing the Tarrant County Bar Association.
—Photo courtesy Wade McMullen

award. In thanking the newspaper for the award and its attendant good publicity, McMullen said, "You have a profession where it's always an adversarial situation, and, in any case, fifty percent of the people are upset with the result and they blame the lawyers." He added, "Also, being in a profession where advertising your services is often frowned upon, tooting one's own horn attracts disdain."[9]

A shining example of President McMullen's idea of a lawyer who gives of himself to his community is Bob Kaman. The 1996 Texas Wesleyan University School of Law graduate was recognized in 1998 by the TCBA and Legal Services for his *pro bono* work. In addition to his "day job" as director of special school programs in the Office of Multicultural Affairs, and teaching students about legal issues in medical practice, Kaman completed fifty-one *pro bono* cases that year.

The biochemist/lawyer noted his law school training taught him how to think differently and see more immediate results than his previous work in the field of pure science. "Now, for the first time in my life, I can sit down face to face and help someone and help resolve a problem," he said.[10]

The September 27, 1998, *Star-Telegram* noted, "Aside from the thousands of hours individual lawyers provide in *pro bono publico* (for the public good) services, the bar association as a group has been quietly undertaking more community service projects."[11]

Cited were support of the West Texas Legal Service, a "Coat and Warm Clothing Drive," and an alcohol awareness program at area high schools.

In a later interview, President Wade McMullen revealed that "$10,000 had been donated to Cook Children's Hospital."[12]

Many of the children come from impoverished families, and that money is used to buy personal necessities such as toothbrushes and other hygiene items, underwear, or needed clothing. A recent project is the placing of boxes in law offices for the hospital. When Cook sends out a "wish list" for needed items, Bar members fill the boxes and take them to the young patients.

In exchange for volunteering their time and money, member attorneys benefit from mentoring and networking. They also receive the *Tarrant County Bar Bulletin*, a monthly publication containing news of events, articles about members of the legal community, library updates, and recent court decisions.

The October 1998 issue contained a feature on the little known career of a former president of the TCBA.

"A quiet man, unassumingly going about his law practice here, helped break an espionage plot that once threatened the nation. He is Allen Conner, local attorney, 1937 class president of Poly High School and an ex-FBI agent."[13]

The story told of his World War II trapping of Nazi spy Fritz Duquesne. His feat became the basis for the movie *The House on 42nd Street*. After leaving the FBI, Conner returned to Fort Worth and practiced with the firm of James & Conner. Conner was president of the Bar in 1953.

Basking in the glow of public recognition by the local newspaper, but not content with their efforts, additional TCBA services were started. "These new projects include a Jury Symposium II, a joint effort with Cooks Children's Hospital called 'Kids Closet,' a new joint project with the (Wesleyan) Law School, a Volunteerism Summit to take place in the spring, a Disaster Relief Assistance Program, and a program called Keep Justice Alive," McMullen wrote in the November 1998 *TCBA Bulletin*.[14] This program, he explained, was a statewide educational effort to highlight positive aspects of the legal profession. In Fort Worth, high school students spent a day in Judge Bob McGrath's 342nd District Court, observing a trial in progress and having an opportunity to interact with the judge. He told the young people, "Through public education like this, lawyers can counter the media's images and demonstrate the good they do in the community."[15]

President McMullen, in an earlier interview, explained his philosophy this way: "One of my mentors once said that we are all like 'Turtles on a Fence Post.' As kids, we all wondered how that turtle got up on the fence post. We've learned over the years that it didn't get up there by itself; it had a lot of help, just like each of us."[16] He went on to admonish lawyers to lend a helping hand for the good of the community.

Roland Johnson, chair of the Alcohol Awareness Committee, with a lawyer-like disclaimer of boasting, outlined some of the achievements of that group. "The Tarrant County Bar Association (TCBA) organized an alcohol-awareness program for over 4,000 high school students and parents in Tarrant County. The TCBA collaborated with the Tarrant County Juvenile Court, the Tarrant County District Attorney's office, the Tarrant County Council on Alcoholism, and the Fort Worth ISD to sponsor an alcohol-awareness program entitled 'It Won't Happen to Me.'"[17] Students saw the programs in their schools, and parents saw the programs through their Parent Teacher Associations.

Part of the program was the Tarrant County Medical Examiner's office report on the health effects of alcohol abuse. Representatives from the district attorney's office gave current information on the new "Zero Tolerance" laws and the consequences of being a juvenile in the criminal justice system. Most chilling was the account of Ms. Ann Lewis, whose father was killed by a drunken driver. "Although the impact of the program could not be measured, the program was presented in the spring of the year [1998] because of ongoing proms and graduation ceremonies. Ms. Ann Lewis stated in her presentation, 'If this program keeps only one of you from drinking and driving, then it's worth it.'"[18]

The Tarrant County Bar Association, in order to recognize lawyers who have exemplified outstanding professionalism in the practice of law, in 1963 established the "Blackstone Award." This award "is presented annually by the Tarrant County Bar Association to a Tarrant County lawyer who exemplifies those attributes most highly prized and cherished by the legal profession. The selection of the awardee is made solely on the basis of consistent ability, integrity, and courage as a lawyer. No other attainment or activities, civil, political, religious, military, social, or otherwise, are considered."[19]

Honorees must be lawyers sixty-five years of age or older, who have practiced in Tarrant County for at least fifteen years, including the previous five years of continuous practice.

A companion award, the "Silver Gavel," was established in 1996 to recognize a noteworthy jurist. "The Silver Gavel Award is to be presented annually by the Tarrant County Bar Association to a Tarrant County jurist who exemplifies an outstanding reputation for competency, efficiency, and integrity."[20] A committee of local attorneys selects both the Silver Gavel and Blackstone Award recipients.

The emphasis on professionalism was the underpinning of the establishment in 1992 of the Eldon B. Mahon Inn of Court. Named for distinguished Judge Mahon, it is an adoption of the English Inns of Court method of mentoring young lawyers and third-year law students. "Dedicated to improving the skills, professionalism, civility, and ethics of the bench and bar, American Inns now total more than 300 active Inns in 49 states and the District of Columbia, encompassing nearly 20,000 members."[21]

The Fort Worth unit's eighty-five members are divided into three categories. "Masters" must have at least fifteen years experience; "Barristers" include lawyers with four to fifteen years experience; "Associates" are lawyers with fewer than four years experience. All must be exemplary in character, ability, and competence. "Pupils" are Texas Wesleyan University School of Law seniors who are nominated by the faculty as having exceptional abilities and promise. The purpose is to help future lawyers improve their skills and sharpen their ethical awareness by having one-on-one learning opportunities with experienced judges and lawyers.

What will the future be for the TCBA? McMullen, looking into his crystal ball, sees an increased focus on educating the community, using advanced technology, and networking with other professional organizations in order to improve the lives not only of lawyers, but of the community as a whole.

The avenue that connects the law school to the courthouse is composed of bricks. Every brick is important to the smooth running of society's vehicle. Embossed on each brick is the memory of a professor who cared enough to demand quality classroom preparation, the memory of seemingly small cases that were important to clients, the memory of the carefully crafted brief, the memory of making the community a better place to live and work, and the satisfaction of being admired for one's honesty and integrity—these are the bricks on which lawyers travel.

Endnotes

Introduction

1. Henry C. Black, *Black's Law Dictionary, Fifth Edition* (St. Paul, MN: West Publishing Co., 1979), 796.

2. *Fort Worth Star-Telegram* (hereinafter FWST) 11/29/58 P.M., 1.

The Early Years

1. Quentin McGown, Speech at dedication of Texas Wesleyan University School of Law, November 15, 1997.

2. Julia Kathryn Garrett, *Fort Worth: A Frontier Triumph* (Austin, TX: The Encino Press, 1972), 125.

3. Quentin McGown, *op. cit.*

4. Federal Writers' Project, *Research Data, Fort Worth and Tarrant County, Texas* Vol. 2 (Fort Worth, TX: Texas Writers' Project, 1941), 632.

5. *Ibid.*, 316.

6. J. C. Terrell, *Reminiscences of the Early Days of Fort Worth* (Fort Worth, TX: Texas Printing Co., 1906), 5.

7. Oliver Knight, *Fort Worth: Outpost on the Trinity* (Fort Worth, TX: Texas Christian University Press, 1990), 27.

8. J. C. Terrell, *op. cit.*, 10.

9. Leonard Sanders and Ronnie Tyler, *How Fort Worth Became the Texasmost City* (Fort Worth, TX: Amon Carter Museum of Western Art, 1973), 36.

10. B. B. Paddock, *History of Texas; Fort Worth and the Texas Northwest* Vol. 1 (Chicago and New York: Lewis Publishing Co., 1922), 195.

11. Richard F. Selcer, *Hell's Half Acre*, No. 9 Chisholm Trail Series (Fort Worth, TX: Texas Christian University Press, 1985), 42.

12. Sanders and Tyler, *op. cit.*, 37.

13. Federal Writers' Project, *op. cit.* Vol. 38, 14,830.

14. Paddock, *op. cit.* Vol. 2, 691.

15. Federal Writers' Project, *op. cit.*, Vol. 3, 1180.

16. *Ibid.*

17. *The Book of Fort Worth* (Fort Worth: Fort Worth Record, 1913), 59.

18. Caleb Pirtle, III, *Fort Worth: The Civilized West* (Tulsa, OK: Continental Heritage Press, Inc., 1980), 40.

19. *Fort Worth City Directory, 1888-1889* (Galveston, TX: Morrison & Fourney, 1889), 13.

20. Federal Writers' Project, *op. cit.* Vol. 4, 1,178.

21. *The Book of Fort Worth*, 60.

22. *Ibid.*

23. Knight, *op. cit.*, 69.

24. *Ibid.*, 61.

25. Selcer, *op. cit.*, 207

26. Personal Interview with Mrs. Marjorie Dews, daughter of J. R. Black.

27. Janet Smelzer, *Where the West Begins: Fort Worth and Tarrant County* (Northridge, CA: Windsor Publications, Inc., 1985), 115.

Fort Worth University

1. *FWST*, Oct. 30, 1949, A.M. Historical Section, 21.

2. Federal Writers' Project, *op. cit.* Vol. 48, 19,030.

3. *The Dallas Herald*, July 8, 1871 (reprinted Aug. 13, 1962 by Southwest and Genealogy Dept., Fort Worth Public Library).

4. W. P. Webb, Editor, *The Handbook of Texas: A Dictionary of Essential Information* Vol. 1, (Austin, TX: Texas State Historical Ass'n., 1952), 636.

5. Paul Millhouse, *Oklahoma City University* (Muskogee, OK: Oklahoma Heritage Ass'n., Western Heritage Books, 1984), 7.

6. *Ibid.*

7. *Fort Worth Weekly Gazette*, Oct. 17, 1889, 1.

8. *FWST*, Oct. 30, 1949 A.M, Historical Section, 21.

9. Mack Williams, *The News Tribune In Old Fort Worth* (Fort Worth, TX: Mack and Madeline Williams, 1976), 110.

10. Scott Barker personal letter to Fort Worth Public Library librarian Ken Hopkins.

11. Federal Writers' Project, *op. cit.* Vol. 34, 13,442.

12. Williams, *op. cit.*, 110.

13. Paul Millhouse, *op. cit.*, 10.

14. *The Lasso*, (FWU Yearbook, 1898), Front matter.

15. Ray Miller, *Ray Miller's Eyes of Texas Series; Fort Worth and the Brazos Valley* Second Edition (Houston, TX: Gulf Publishing Co., 1992), 125.

16. Millhouse, *op. cit.*, 10.

17. *The Fort Worth Record*, May 26, 1911, 8.

18. Barker letter to Hopkins.

19. *Texas Bar Journal* Vol. 11 (Sept. 1948): 518.

20. *Ibid.*, Vol. 61 (Dec. 1953): 767.

21. *Fort Worth Press* (hereinafter *Press*), Sept. 12, 1960, 32.

22. Millhouse, *op. cit.*, 240.

23. *Ibid.*, 262.

24. *Twenty-ninth Catalog of Fort Worth University* (Fort Worth: Keystone Pub. Co., 1909), 30.

Non-Traditional Study of the Law

1. *Fort Worth Record*, Jan. 17, 1915, 4.

2. *Ibid.*

3. Federal Writers' Project, *op. cit.* Vol. 40, 15,641.
4. *Ibid.*
5. *FWST*, Sept. 14, 1938 P.M., 1.
6. *Ibid.*, Jan. 16, 1938 P.M., 4.
7. Bennett Smith, *Tarrant County Bar Memorials: 1938-1976* (Fort Worth, TX: self-published, 1977) 106.
8. Knight, *op. cit.*, 276.

Texas Christian University School of Law

1. Williams, *op. cit.*, 111.
2. Pirtle, III, *op. cit.*, 103.
3. *The Book of Fort Worth*, 60.
4. Colby Hall, *History of Texas Christian University* (Fort Worth, TX: Texas Christian University Press, 1947), 159.
5. Jerome Moore, *TCU: A Hundred Years* (Fort Worth, TX: Texas Christian University Press, 1974), 80.
6. E. R. Cockrell, "Our Law School and Its Future," in *The Skiff,* (TCU's student newspaper) Mar. 29, 1918, 3.
7. *The Skiff*, Sept. 28, 1917, 1.
8. *Ibid.*, Sept. 17, 1920, 1.
9. Moore, *op. cit.*, 80.
10. Hall, *op. cit.*, 158.
11. *Ibid.*, 161.
12. *FWST*, June 17, 1967 A.M., 1.
13. *Texas Bar Journal* Vol. 30 (Nov. 1967): 929.

The Jefferson School of Law

1. Gladys Shannon, editor, *The Jeffersonian; 1932 Yearbook*, 32.
2. Shannon, *op. cit.*, 9.
3. *Ibid.*, 39.
4. *Ibid.*, 33.
5. Personal interview with Judge Eva Bloore Barnes.
6. *Ibid.*
7. *Ibid.*
8. *Press*, Apr. 6, 1958, 40.
9. *Ibid.*, Feb. 1, 1962, 6.
10. *Ibid.*, Feb. 16, 1964, 4B.
11. *FWST*, May 13, 1962 A.M., Section 4, 20.
12. Judge Barnes's personal papers.
13. Personal interview with George Gleeson, Jr.
14. Gleeson, Jr.'s personal papers.
15. *Ibid.*
16. *Texas Bar Journal*, Vol. 4 (July 1941): 386.
17. *Ibid.*, Vol. 33 (April 1970): 315.
18. Shannon, *op. cit.*, 37.
19. *Ibid.*, 32.

The North Texas School of Law

1. Thomas Murphy's personal document.
2. Personal interview with Thomas Murphy.
3. *Ibid.*
4. *Ibid.*
5. Federal Writers' Project, *op. cit.* Vol.36, 14,135.
6. Murphy, personal interview.
7. Federal Writers' Project, *op. cit.* Vol.36, 14,136.
8. *Ibid.*, 14,135.
9. FWST, Oct. 16, 1948 P.M., 1.
10. Smith, *op. cit.*, 260.
11. FWST, Feb. 15, 1951 P.M., 1.
12. Personal interview with J. Olcott Phillips.
13. *Texas Bar Journal*, Vol. 34 (Oct. 1971): 934.
14. *Ibid.*
15. *Ibid.*, Vol. 38 (Apr. 1975): 377.
16. *Ibid.*
17. FWST, Jan. 19, 1975 A.M., 16A.
18. *Ibid.*, Aug. 1, 1948 A.M., 8.

The Dallas/Fort Worth School of Law

1. Personal interview with Karen Chaney, widow of Steve Chaney.
2. *FWST*, Nov. 5, 1996, 2B.
3. Personal interview with Robert "Bob" Harmon.
4. Personal interview with Nancy Berger.
5. Personal interview with Frank Elliott.
6. Rachel S. Master, *The Business Press*, May 6, 1994, 4.
7. Personal interview with Gary Cumbie.
8. *Ibid.*
9. Master, *op. cit.*, May 6, 1994.

Texas Wesleyan University School of Law

1. Thomas Armstrong, editor, *Wesleyan 2001: A Planning Odyssey*. Nov. 15, 1996, 2.
2. Undated brochure: History section; Texas Wesleyan University publication.
3. *Wesleyan: An Official Publication of Texas Wesleyan University*, Summer 1997, 2.
4. *Ibid.*, 3.
5. Bill Teeter, *FWST*, July 22, 1992 A.M., 13A.
6. Lydia Lum, *FWST*, June 16, 1994 A.M., 32A.
7. Linda Campbell *FWST*, Nov. 5, 1995 A. M. 2B.
8. *The Rambler* (Texas Wesleyan University student newspaper), Vol. 79, #20, Nov. 6, 1996, 1.
9. Bill Teeter, *FWST*, Aug. 11, 1994 A.M., 21A.
10. *FWST*, Oct. 12, 1994 A.M., 21A.
11. *Ibid.*, Oct. 28, 1995 A.M., 38A.

12. *Ibid.*

13. *Ibid.*, Aug. 26, 1997 A.M., 2B.

14. *Programs, Policies & Procedures; Texas Wesleyan University School of Law. 1998-1999*, 45.

15. *Ibid.*

16. Personal interview with James Hambleton

17. Hambleton speech, "Information Technology and Globization: The Future of American Legal Education." Nov. 15, 1997.

18. *Programs, Policies & Procedures*, 45.

19. *Law Library Guide* (Texas Wesleyan University, Spring 1999), 11.

20. *Programs, Policies & Procedures*, 5.

21. *Texas Wesleyan University School of Law, 1997-98*, 1.

22. *Ibid.*

23. *Programs, Policies & Procedures*, 9.

24. Personal interview with Kleber Miller.

25. Personal interview with Malinda Seymore.

26. Personal interview with Gary Cumbie.

27. Quentin McGown, "Texas Wesleyan Law School Granted Full ABA Approval." *Wesleyan*, Fall 1999/Winter 2000, 11.

The Courthouses

1. Mike Moncrief, *House of Courts* (Fort Worth: Joe M. Walker, Ward Bogard, 1983), {pages not numbered.}

2. June R. Welch, and Larry J. Nance, *The Texas Courthouses* (Dallas, TX: Yellow Rose Press, 1971), 322.

3. Knight, *Outpost on the Trinity*, 35.

4. Paddock, *North and West Texas*, 205.

5. *Ibid.*, 206.

6. Knight, *op. cit.*, 36.

7. Dee Barker, letter to County Judge Tom Vandergriff, Feb. 1, 1995.

8. *FWST*, Oct. 30, 1949 A.M, Historical Section, 21.

9. Terrell, *Reminiscences*, 20.

10. Judge Stephen King's personal papers.

11. *Ibid.*

12. Sanders, *How Fort Worth Became*, 31.

13. *Ibid.*, 40.

14. Quentin McGown speech, Nov. 15, 1997.

15. Barker letter in King's personal papers.

16. Sanders, *op. cit.*, 44.

17. Steve M. King, *The Tarrant County Courthouse: A Self-Guided Walking Tour* (1996): 3.

18. *Ibid.*

19. Williams, *In Old Fort Worth*, 72.

20. Barker letter to Tom Vandergriff.

21. King, *op. cit.*, 2.

22. *FWST*, July 24, 1941 P.M., 9.

23. Frank Evans, *Press*, Sept. 8, 1944, 1.

24. *FWST*, Sept. 25, 1952 P.M., 38.

25. *Ibid.*, Apr. 18, 1960 P.M., 1.

26. *Ibid.*, Dec. 21, 1994 P.M., 17.
27. *Ibid.*, Oct. 29, 1954 P.M., 19.
28. *Ibid.*
29. Linda Campbell, *FWST*, Mar. 23, 1999, 11A.
30. Williams, *Fort Worth News Tribune*, Dec. 2, 1983, 1.
31. Neil Strassman, *FWST*, Mar. 24, 1999, 1B.
32. Moncrief, *op.cit.*

Carnage at the Courthouse

1. *FWST*, July 2, 1992, A.M., 18A.
2. *Ibid.*
3. *Ibid.*
4. *Ibid.*
5. *Ibid.*
6. Todd Copilevitz, *Dallas Morning News*, Feb. 14, 1993, 17A.
7. *FWST*, July 2, 1992, A.M., 20A.
8. *Ibid.*, 1A.
9. *Ibid.*, 18A.
10. *Ibid.*, Feb. 14, 1993 A.M., 17A.
10. *Ibid.*
11. *Ibid.*
12. *FWST*, Sept. 20, 1994 A.M., 1A.
13. *Ibid.*, July 2, 1992 A.M., 19A.

The Texas Supreme Court

1. *The Rambler*, Mar. 10, 1999, 1.
2. *Ibid.*
3. Personal interview with hearing spectator.
4. *FWST*, Mar. 5, 1999, 6B.
5. *Ibid.*
6. *Ibid.*
7. Personal notes from observation of hearing.
8. *FWST*, Mar. 5, 1999, 6B.
9. *Ibid.*
10. *The Rambler*, Mar. 10, 1999, 1.
11. *FWST*, Mar. 5, 1999, 1B.
12. *The Rambler*, Mar. 10, 1999, 1.
13. *Ibid.*
14. *Ibid.*

The Frederick A. Cook Oil Scandal

1. Roger and Diana Olien, *Oil Promoters and Investors in the Jazz Age; Easy Money* (Chapel Hill, NC: University of North Carolina Press, 1990), 74.
2. Hugh Eames, *Winner Lose All: Dr. Cook & the Theft of the North Pole* (Boston: Little, Brown and Company, 1973), 8.
3. *Ibid.*, 287.
4. *Ibid.*, 289.

5. *Press*, Nov. 9, 1922, 1.
6. *United States v Cook*, Federal Court Record, Case #2273.
7. Pirtle, III, *Fort Worth: The Civilized West*, 116.
8. Case #2273, grand jury filing, 1.
9. *Ibid.*, 2.
10. *Ibid.*, 3.
11. *Ibid.*, 5.
12. *Ibid.*, 7.
13. Roger Olien, *op. cit.*, 133.
14. *Ibid.*, 134.
15. Black, *Black's Law Dictionary*, 149.
16. Case #2273, *op. cit.*
17. *Press*, Oct. 27, 1923, 1.
18. Roger Olien, *op. cit.*, 136.
19. *Dallas Morning News*, Oct. 16, 1923.
20. *FWST*, Nov. 8, 1923 Home Edition, 4.
21. Case #2273, Vol. 25, Nov. 22, 1923, 147.
22. *Ibid.*,163.
23. *Ibid.*, 166.
24. *Ibid.*, 173.
25. *Ibid.*
26. *FWST*, Nov. 14, 1923 Home Edition, 1.
27. Harold Abramson, *Hero in Disgrace: The Life of Arctic Explorer, Frederick A. Cook* (New York: Parago House, 1991), 193.
28. *Ibid.*
29. *Ibid.*, 195.
30. Eames, *op. cit.*, 295.
31. *Ibid.*, 298.
32. *Ibid.*, 300.
33. *FWST*, Nov. 21, 1923 Home Edition, 1.

The J. Frank Norris Murder Trial

1. Barry Hankins, *God's Rascal: J. Frank Norris and the Beginnings of Southern Fundamentalism* (Lexington, KY: The University of Kentucky Press, 1996), 118.
2. Pirtle, III, *op. cit.*, 92.
3. Hankins, *op. cit.*, 16.
4. *FWST*, Jan. 24, 1924 P.M., 1.
5. Hankins, *op. cit.*, 127.
6. *Ibid.*, 119.
7. *FWST*, Jan. 14, 1927 P.M., 1.
8. Federal Writers' Project, *op. cit.* Vol. 33, 1314.
9. Roy E. Falls, *A Fascinating Biography of J. Frank Norris* (Euless, TX: self published, 1975), 61.
10. Verbatim Testimony, *Fort Worth Record-Telegram*, Jan. 21, 1927 City Edition, 10.
11. *Ibid.*, 8.
12. *Ibid.*, 9.
13. *Ibid.*, 23.

14. *Ibid.*
15. *Ibid.*, 8.
16. *Ibid.*, Jan. 21, 1927, 1.
17. *Ibid.*, Jan. 26, 1927,6.
18. *Ibid.*
19. Federal Writers' Project,*op. cit.* Vol. 35, 13,821.
20. Falls, *op. cit.*, 68.

The Legacy of Oil Money

1. Sylvia Jones, editor, *Wilbarger Centennial Commemorative Book: 1881-1981* (Vernon, TX: Wilbarger Centennial Association, 1981), 50.
2. H. H. Halsell, *Cowboys and Cattleland* (Fort Worth, TX: Texas Christian University Press, 1983), 223.
3. Frank Reeves, "Operating Policy of Three-D's Is Unchanged" *FWST*, July 10, 1955 A. M. Farm and Ranch Section, 6.
4. *W. T. Waggoner Estate v Lula Judd Wharton* 46th District Court Case #12,511, 3.
5. *Ibid.*, Section 5, 4.
6. *Ibid.*, 5.
7. *Ibid.*
8. 46th District Court Case # 12, 249: Supplemental Finding of Fact No. 37, 1369.
9. *Ibid.*, Finding of Fact No. 38, 1369.
10. *Ibid.*, Finding of Fact No. 45, 1375.
11. *Ibid.*, Finding of Fact No. 47, 1373.
12. *Vernon Daily Record*, Mar. 29, 1967, 1.
13. *Ibid.*
14. *Ibid.*
15. 46th District Court Cause No. 19,626, Mar. 13, 1996.
16. Judge Tom Neely letter to E. Glen Johnson, Jan. 18, 1996.

The Trailblazers

1. Selcer, *Hell's Half Acre*, 272.
2. *Fort Worth Record and Register*, Mar. 23, 1907, 1.
3. *Ibid.*
4. Pirtle, III, *op. cit.*, 90.
5. *Fort Worth Record and Register*, Mar. 23, 1907, 1.
6. J. A. "Tiny" Gooch, in-house historian, *100 Years: Cantey, Hanger, Gooch, Munn & Collins*, pages not numbered; page numbers approximated, 1.
7. *Ibid.*, 3.
8. *Ibid.*, 6.
9. *Ibid.*
10. *Ibid.*, 8.
11. *Ibid.*, 10.
12. Personal interview with Perry Cockerell.
13. Pirtle, III, *op. cit.*, 210.
14. Quentin McGown's personal papers.
15. *Ibid.*

16. *Ibid.*
17. *Ibid.*

Legendary Lawyers

1. Mabel Gouldy, *FWST*, Dec. 15, 1957 A.M., 8.
2. *FWST*, Nov. 29, 1958 P.M., 1.
3. *Ibid.*
4. *Ibid.*, July 12, 1948 A.M., 10.
5. *Ibid.*
6. *Ibid.*, Nov. 6, 1954 P.M., 7
7. Sidney Samuels, "Love of Liberty," *Vital Speeches of the Day* Vol. 6, No. 9 (Feb. 15, 1940): 272.
8. *FWST*, Dec. 17, 1957 A.M., 1.
9. *Ibid.*, Nov. 30, 1958 A.M., 14.
10. *Ibid.*
11. Personal interview with Forrest Markward.
12. Linda Campbell, *FWST*, Jan. 1. 1999, 1B.
13. *Ibid.*
14. Personal interview with Forrest Markward.
15. Tarrant County Bar Association Archives.
16. *Tarrant County Bar Association Bulletin* (hereinafter *TCBAB*), Vol. 9, No. 15 (Apr. 1999): 4.
17. *Ibid.*
18. *Ibid.*, 5.
19. *Ibid.*
20. Telephone interview with Winfred Hooper.
21. *FWST*, Apr. 14, 1999, 3B.
22. *TCBAB*, Vol. 9, No. 15 (Apr. 1999): 5.
23. Personal interview with Kleber Miller.
24. *Ibid.*
25. Personal interview with L. Clifford Davis.

Lawyers and Politics

1. *FWST*, Aug. 1, 1948 A.M., 8.
2. *Ibid.*, Jan. 19, 1975 A.M. 8.
3. Personal interview with Joe Spurlock II.
4. *Ibid.*
5. *Ibid.*
6. *Ibid.*
7. *Dallas Morning News*, July 25, 1982, 4.
8. *Ibid.*
9. Personal interview with Don Gladden.
10. *News-Tribune*, Nov. 18, 1977, 9.
11. *Ibid.*
12. Personal interview with Don Gladden.

The Tarrant County Bar Association

1. *TCBAB* Vol. 9, No. 8 (Aug. 1998): 3.
2. Tarrant County Bar Association Archives 1937 letter.
3. *FWST*, May 28, 1960 A.M., 12.
4. *The Bar News* Vol. 27, No. 6 (Feb. 1969): 1.
5. *TCBAB* Vol. 9, No. 10 (Oct. 1998): 4.
6. *Tarrant County Bar Association 1997-1998 Directory*, 10.
7. Personal interview with Wade McMullen.
8. *Ibid.*
9. *FWST*, Sept. 27, 1998 Special Feature Club Directory, 27.
10. Linda Campbell, *FWST*, Dec. 9, 1998 3B.
11. *FWST*, Sept. 27, 1998 Club Directory, 27.
12. Personal interview with Wade McMullen.
13. *TCBAB* Vol. 9, No. 10 (Oct. 1998): 9.
14. *Ibid.* Vol. 9, No. 11 (Nov. 1998): 3.
15. *Ibid.*, 5.
16. *Ibid.* Vol. 9, No. 7 (July 1998): 3.
17. *Ibid.* Vol. 9, No. 10 (Oct. 1998): 3.
18. *Ibid.*
19. *Bar Association 1997-1998 Directory* 13.
20. *Ibid.*
21. *TCBAB* Vol. 9, No. 10 (Oct. 1998): 13.

Bibliography

Reference Works

Black, Henry C. *Black's Law Dictionary*. Fifth Edition. St. Paul, MN: West Publishing Co., 1979.

Federal Writers' Project. *Research Data, Fort Worth and Tarrant County Texas*. Seventy volumes. Ft. Worth: Texas Writers' Project, 1941.

Paddock, B. B. *History of Texas: Fort Worth and the Texas Northwest Edition*. Four volumes. Chicago: Lewis Publishing Co., 1922.

Smith, Bennett L. *Tarrant County Bar Memorials: 1938-1976*. Ft. Worth: Self published, 1977.

Tyler, Ron *et al*., Editor. *The New Handbook of Texas*. Six volumes. Austin, TX: Texas State Historical Association, 1996.

Webb, W. P., et al., Editor. *The Handbook of Texas: A Dictionary of Essential Information*. Austin, TX: Texas State Historical Association, 1952.

Books

Abramson, Howard S. *Hero in Disgrace: The Life of Arctic Explorer Frederick A. Cook*. New York: Paragon House, 1991.

Eames, Hugh. *Winner Lose All: Dr. Cook & the Theft of the North Pole*. Boston: Little, Brown and Company, 1973.

Falls, Roy E. *A Fascinating Biography of J. Frank Norris*. Euless, TX: P.O. Box 179, Euless, TX 76039. Self-published, 1975.

Garrett, Julia Kathryn. *Fort Worth: A Frontier Triumph*. Austin, TX: The Encino Press, 1972.

Hall, Colby D. *History of Texas Christian University*. Ft. Worth: Texas Christian University Press, 1947.

Hankins, Barry. *God's Rascal: J. Frank Norris and the Beginnings of Southern Fundamentalism*. Lexington, KY: The University of Kentucky Press, 1996.

Jones, Sylvia, Editor. *Wilbarger Centennial Commemorative Book: 1881-1981*. Vernon, TX: Wilbarger Centennial Ass'n., 1981.

Knight, Oliver. *Fort Worth: Outpost on the Trinity*. Ft. Worth, TX: Texas Christian University Press, 1990.

Miller, Ray. *Ray Miller's Eyes of Texas Series: Fort Worth and the Brazos Valley*. Second edition. Houston: Gulf Pub. Co., 1992.

Millhouse, Paul. *Oklahoma City University* Oklahoma Horizons Series. Muskogee, OK: Oklahoma Heritage Association Western Heritage Books, 1984.

Moore, Jerome A. *TCU: A Hundred Years of History*. Ft. Worth: Texas Christian University Press, 1974.

Olien, Roger M. and Olien, Diana Davids. *Oil Promoters and Investors in the Jazz Age: Easy Money*. Chapel Hill, NC: University of North Carolina Press, 1990.

Pirtle, Caleb, III. *Fort Worth: The Civilized West*. Tulsa, OK: Continental Heritage Press, Inc., 1980.

Porter, Roze. *Thistle Hill: The Cattle Baron's Legacy*. Ft. Worth: Branch-Smith, Inc., 1980.

Ritchie, Homer G. *The Life and Legend of J. Frank Norris, "The Fighting Parson."* Ft. Worth, 7314 Durango Dr. Ft. Worth, TX 76179, 1991.

Sanders, Leonard and Tyler, Ronnie C. *How Fort Worth Became the Texasmost City*. Ft. Worth: Amon Carter Museum of Western Art, 1973.

Selcer, Richard F. *Hell's Half Acre* No. 9, Chisholm Trail Series. Ft. Worth: Texas Christian University Press, 1991.

Smelzer, Janet L. *Where the West Begins: Fort Worth and Tarrant County*. Northridge, CA: Windsor Publications, Inc., 1985.

Terrell, J. C. *Reminiscences of the Early Days of Fort Worth*. Ft. Worth: Texas Printing Co., 1906.

Welch, June Rayfield, and Nance, J. Larry. *The Texas Courthouse*. Dallas: Yellow Rose Press, 1971.

Williams, Mack, and Williams, Madeline, Editors. *The News Tribune In Old Fort Worth*. Ft. Worth: Mack and Madeline Williams, 1976.

Periodicals and Yearbooks

The Horned Frog. Texas Christian University Yearbook.
The Jeffersonian. Jefferson School of Law Yearbook.
The Lasso. Fort Worth University Yearbook.
Texas Bar Journal.
Tarrant County Bar Association Bulletin.
Tarrant County Bar Association Directory.
Vital Speeches of the Day.
Wesleyan. Texas Wesleyan University Quarterly.

Newspapers

The Dallas Morning News.
The (Ft. Worth) *Business Press*.
Fort Worth Press.
Fort Worth Record.
Fort Worth Register.
Fort Worth Record and Register.
Fort Worth Record-Telegram.
Fort Worth Star-Telegram.
Fort Worth Weekly Gazette.
The Rambler. Texas Wesleyan University student newspaper.
The Skiff. Texas Christian University student newspaper.
Vernon (Texas) *Daily Record*.

Public Records

United States of America v F. A. Cook, et al., Case 2273. District Court of the United States, Northern District of Texas, Fort Worth Division. On deposit in Federal Records Center, Fort Worth, TX. Cook's trial pleadings and testimony fill Volumes 23, 25 and 26.

W. T. Waggoner Estate v Lula Judd Wharton, Case No. 12,511. District Court of Wilbarger County, Texas, 46th Judicial District. Findings 37, 38, 45 and 47. Waggoner Estate documents on deposit in Wilbarger County Clerk's office, Vernon, TX.

Private Papers and Unpublished Works

Barker, Scott. Personal letter to Ken Hopkins, Genealogy and Local History Manager. Ft. Worth Public Library, dated March 22, 1997.

Cantey and Hanger LLP unpublished history of the firm, 100 Years.

Cause No. 19,626, W. T. Waggoner Estate, Motion to Retain, March 13, 1996.

Fort Worth City Directory, 1888-1889. On microfiche, Ft. Worth Public Library, Genealogy and Local History Department.

Twenty-ninth Catalog of Fort Worth University. Ft. Worth Public Library, Genealogy and Local History Department.

Gleeson, George, Jr. Personal papers.

King, Judge Steve M. Personal papers. Dee Barker memo to County Judge Tom Vandergriff.

Law Library Guide, Texas Wesleyan University School of Law pamphlet.

McGown, Quentin, IV. Personal papers.

Murphy, Thomas. Personal papers.

Texas Wesleyan University brochure, "History," undated, no author listed.

Wesleyan 2001: A Planning Guide, limited distribution document; Texas Wesleyan University.

Interviews

Barnes, Judge Eva Bloore, retired judge, Jefferson Law School graduate.

Berger, Nancy, attorney, Texas Wesleyan University School of Law graduate.

Chaney, Karen, widow of Steve Chaney.

Cockerell, Perry, attorney, Cantey and Hanger LLP.

Cumbie, Gary, Texas Wesleyan University Board of Trustees member.

Davis, Judge L. Clifford.

Dews, Marjorie, daughter of Judge J. R. Black.

Elliott, Frank, professor, Texas Wesleyan University School of Law, former dean, Dallas/Ft. Worth Law School.

Gladden, Don, attorney, 1999 Blackstone Award recipient.

Gleeson, George, Jr., son of Jefferson University Law School graduate,

Hambleton, James, Director, Texas Wesleyan University School of Law Library.

Harmon, Robert, founder of Dallas/Ft. Worth Law School.

Harris, Nelda, attorney.

Hooper, Winfield, attorney, 1999 Blackstone Award recipient.

Markward, Forrest, retired attorney.

McMullen, Wade, attorney, 1998-1999 TCBA president.

McGown, Quentin, IV, Texas Wesleyan University historian and law student.
Miller, Kleber, attorney.
Murphy, Thomas, retired attorney, North Texas Law School graduate.
Phillips, J. Olcott, retired attorney, North Texas Law School graduate.
Seymore, Malinda, associate dean, Texas Wesleyan University School of Law.
Spurlock, Joe II, professor, Texas Wesleyan University School of Law

Notes from Personal Observations

Nov. 15, 1997, Texas Wesleyan University School of Law dedication ceremony and seminar.
Mar. 4, 1999, Texas Supreme Court hearings held at Texas Wesleyan University School of Law.

Index